Early Praise For *The Startup Student*

"I love working with students because of their boundless energy and optimism. But too many of them become discouraged when they hit predictable roadblocks. We see the same patterns each and every semester. *The Startup Student* is a candid, practical, and tactical guide to help the aspiring student entrepreneurs navigate these roadblocks. Students can't change the world if their idea never comes to life. *The Startup Student* will put them on the right path forward."

–Diana Kander
New York Times Best Selling Author of *All In Startup*

"*The Startup Student* is a great read for any entrepreneur or any student, but for every entrepreneurship student it's really more of a bible! It's THE book I wish I had back when I was a student! The insight provided is valuable, timely, and specifically contextualized to aspiring student entrepreneurs. Eric Liguori and the 20+ other entrepreneurial thought leaders hit the nail on the head by laying out practical, real-world advice to not only help you ensure entrepreneurial success, but also avoid a few landmines along the way."

–Steve Kaplan
New York Times Best Selling Author of
Be the Elephant and *Bag the Elephant*

"*The Startup Student* is the best resource I have seen for future or current college entrepreneurs. This is not a textbook, it is your framework for how to get the most out of your college education. I was fortunate to get involved with my school's entrepreneurship program and student club beginning the first day of my freshman year, and have lived the startup student life for 4 years. The advice and experience packed into this quick read is invaluable!"

–Connor Alstrom
Fresno State Entrepreneurship Club President (2013-2015)

"*The Startup Student* is a fantastic book that provides students with highly necessary advice from the real-world perspective of a student entrepreneur. The content is fresh, honest, and practical, making it especially relevant to those looking to make their entrepreneurial dreams a reality. I wish I had this book in my hands during my studies!"

–Dr. Olli Vuola
Executive Director, Aalto Ventures Program, Finland

The Startup Student

Also by Eric Liguori

Entrepreneurship: Venture Initiation, Management, and Development, 2nd Edition
(with George Vozikis, Tim Mescon, and Howard Feldman)

Annals of Entrepreneurship Education & Pedagogy, Vol. 2 (with Michael Morris)

The Startup Student

Practical Advice on How to Succeed
as a Student Entrepreneur

Dr. Eric Liguori

The Startup Student

Copyright © 2016 by Eric Liguori

Published 2016 by Entrepreneurship Education Project Press

Printed in the United States of America

First Edition

Cover and interior design by Duran Hernandez

ISBN-10: 0-9974198-0-6
ISBN-13: 978-0-9974198-0-1

Paperback printing 10 9 8 7 6 5 4 3 2 1

To my family, for everything.

To Mark Weaver, for sending me down the entrepreneurship education path.

To my colleagues, for supporting my crazy ideas.

To the book contributors, for sharing my passion of helping students succeed.

And, to you, the student entrepreneur, for all the great accomplishments
yet to come from your efforts.

Table of Contents

List of Contributors

Ramon Aleman is the Founder and CEO of Unhoused Humanity (www.unhousedhumanity.org), a FL-based nonprofit organization that houses the homeless. Aleman is also an entrepreneurship student at Florida State University and the 2016 winner of the $10,000 inNOLEvation Challenge.

Josh Bendickson is an entrepreneur turned professor on faculty at East Carolina University. He has a background in both corporate recruiting and real estate and serves on both ECU's internship committee and the advisory committee of the new Miller School of Entrepreneurship.

Beth Bridges, The Networking Motivator™, has attended over 2,300 networking events in the last 11 years. Based on this experience, she authored *Networking on Purpose*, a #1 Amazon Best-Selling Business Networking Book in Small Business & Entrepreneurship.

Birton Cowden is the Associate Director of the Berthiaume Center for Entrepreneurship at UMass Amherst (the 2016 National Emerging Undergraduate Entrepreneurship Program Awardee) and is on the faculty of the Isenberg School of Management. Cowden is also a principal n Probst, Inc. and co-founder of EOI.

Aris Creates is an arts entrepreneur specializing in business system development and negotiation. In late 2015 she and Stephen Hnilica founded Backpack Entrepreneurs™ (backpackentrepreneurs.com), and now they travel the globe together running their companies from whatever hostel, sofa, or coffee shop they find.

Evan English Ernst founded Who We Play For (whoweplayfor.org) with some teammates while still a college student and has since built it into the premier national organization working to prevent sudden cardiac arrest in student athletes. As of late 2015, Who We Play For had conducted 65,829 heart screenings and saved the lives of 63 student athletes.

Betsy Hays is a speaker and public relations professor accredited by the Public Relations Society of America. Hays is also the co-author of *Win & Wow: Public Relations Secrets for Everyday Success*, *Land Your Dream Career in College: The Complete Guide to Success*, and *Life After College: 10 Steps to Build a Life You Love*.

Stephen Hnilica is an online marketing specialist with a penchant for adventure and exploration. In late 2015 he and Aris Creates founded Backpack Entrepreneurs™ (www.backpackentrepreneurs.com), and now they travel the globe together running their companies from whatever hostel, sofa, or coffee shop they find.

Greg Horn co-founded Gigawatt, a crowdfunding platform for blitz fundraising, with some fellow Lehigh University alumni in 2012. Now Horn runs 27Ventures, working with inventors, entrepreneurs, investors and non-profits to make their dreams a reality.

Prashant Joshi is a seasoned product launch pro. Presently he works for Lakos as a Business Development Manager where he oversees a team of five responsible for marketing and business development. Prior to joining Lakos, Joshi was Director of Fresno State's Technology Commercialization Program.

Dean A. Koutroumanis is a restaurateur turned educator. Presently he is the Associate Director of the John P. Lowth Entrepreneurship Center at The University of Tampa (the 2016 National Model Undergraduate Entrepreneurship Program awardee). He also owns a commercial real estate investment company and has equity in a Clearwater, FL based restaurant.

Michael Luchies is an entrepreneur and writer. He is the founder of TrepRep (www.treprep.com), where he works with entrepreneurs and small businesses to develop and execute content marketing strategies. With over 1,000 published articles both as a writer and ghostwriter, Luchies has been mentioned or featured in *Fortune*, *Entrepreneur.com*, *Huffington Post*, *Under30CEO*, and the *Breaking Down Your Business* podcast.

Daniel McDonald works with teams to perfect their pitches and slide decks. He's coached entrepreneurs and startup teams competing in the Hult Prize Competition, the Tibetan Innovation Challenge, Startup Weekend, and Global Startup Battle, to name a few, and is a community organizer for 1 Million Cups, a weekly pitch program designed to educate, engage, and connect entrepreneurs.

Chuck Papageorgiou is the Founder and Managing Partner of Ideasphere (http://www.ideasphere.com), which specializes in the high-tech, logistics, and financial services segments. Papageorgiou is also the Co-Founder and CEO of International Screening Solutions, a company providing risk management services to the background screening industry, and serves as the Entrepreneur-In-Residence at both the Lowth Entrepreneurship Center and Moffit Cancer Center.

Mike Pronovost is the Founder of Pronovost Technologies, a technology company that enables high speed Internet and mobile computer access in rural areas. He has been featured in *PC Magazine, Businessweek,* and *Forbes.* Pronovost was named to the national Empact 100 list and received two awards at the White House for technology innovation and entrepreneurship.

Daniel James Scott is Executive Director of the Tampa Bay Technology Forum, co-founder of Alorum, and serves on the board for the Lions Eye Institute for Transplant & Research. Scott co-founded the Entrepreneurship program at USF St. Petersburg, earning him the honors of Association for Small Business and Entrepreneurship's Educator of the Year and the U.S. Small Business Administration's Florida Business Advocate of the Year.

Nelson Sebra is a serial entrepreneur having launched nine businesses, ranging from a BBQ restaurant to a hazardous waste treatment company. Presently Sebra is the Entrepreneur-In-Residence at the Lyles Center for Innovation and Entrepreneurship at Fresno State, where he teaches as well as manages their student incubator.

Patrick Snyder is the Executive Director of the United States Association for Small Business and Entrepreneurship (www.usasbe.org). Snyder's entrepreneurial journey began at age 27 when he grew *Shoreline Magazine* from 2 to 20 employees in just three years, after which he sold the venture.

Katie Sowa is the Senior Director of Startups at Future Founders (www.futurefounders.com) where she leads their collegiate division. Prior to joining Future Founders, Sowa was the Director of Operations for the Collegiate Entrepreneurs' Organization National Office.

Caroline Vanevenhoven's background in the arts gives her a unique mindset and approach to business. With her husband Jeff, she's owned and helped operate a few successful ventures. Today she spends her time raising four kids, one an artist, and the other three hopefully future entrepreneurs.

Jeff Vanevenhoven is an entrepreneur and is on the U.S. Association for Small Business and Entrepreneurship Board of Directors. Vanevenhoven also teaches strategy and entrepreneurship in the College of Business at the University of Wisconsin-Whitewater.

Doan Winkel is Co-Founder of Legacy Out Loud (legacyoutloud.com), a global initiative to refocus the foundational conversations that inspire, empower and give young women the foundation to think and act entrepreneurially; internrocket (internrocket.com), a platform for micro-internships so people can sample lots of different types of work to engineer their dream job; and TEDxNormal. He also teaches entrepreneurship at Illinois State University and shares his unique teaching approach at www.teachinglean.com.

Foreword

Steve Kaplan is a serial entrepreneur and the two-time New York Times Bestselling author of Bag the Elephant and Be the Elephant. Steve is the Founder and President of the World Armwrestling League, the fastest growing sports league in the world now airing on ESPN. He is also a highly sought-after public speaker and business consultant who has appeared on a variety of national media, including ABC's Secret Millionaire. Steve is a Tony-nominated producer for the Broadway production "Leap of Faith." His website is www.stevekaplanlive.com.

The Startup Student is THE book I wish I had when I was a student! The insight provided is valuable, timely, and immediately relevant to aspiring student entrepreneurs. Eric Liguori and the 20+ other entrepreneurial thought leaders hit the nail on the head by laying out practical, real-world advice not only to help you ensure entrepreneurial success, but also to avoid a few landmines along the way. When my friend Patrick Snyder, one of the book's contributors, asked me to write the foreword, I jumped at the opportunity. Seeing students aspire to be entrepreneurs has long been one of the most rewarding parts of my work, second only to being able to start and grow the Kaplan Family Foundation (which, coincidentally, has a similar mission to this book: to help people achieve their dreams by providing resources to help them succeed).

As part of my *Bag the Elephant Unplugged* tour, I had the opportunity to travel the U.S. speaking to college students, faculty, and administrators at Tulane, Cornell, the University of Pennsylvania, Arizona State, Grambling State, the University of Illinois, Penn State, and Depaul. As I spoke on topics like identifying high growth industries, brand differentiation, and learning the language, I was consistently impressed at the high level of business acumen and strong desire to change the world present among today's generation of students but also dismayed at their lack of real-world experience and street IQ. Thankfully, that's where this book, *The Startup Student*, comes in! The pages that follow contain nuggets of wisdom to help you navigate your university experience, build a more entrepreneurial mindset, and get the most bang for your buck out of your student status when launching a new venture. Read the book, take the advice to heart, and believe me when I say this content is time-tested.

Part I of *The Startup Student* challenges you to be bold when coming up with ideas; to solve big problems. Nobel Peace Prize-winner Muhammad Yunus, the father of microfinance whose programs have empowered over 100 million people around the globe to step out of poverty, couldn't have made the impact he did without being bold. As a serial entrepreneur myself, I've never regretted bold thinking, even when outcomes weren't the best. I couldn't have built and ultimately sold SCA as part of a publicly traded company for $2.1 billion without bold thinking; in fact bold thinking is often one of the things I credit a lot of my success to, and is certainly a critical part of ideation.

In Part II, David McCullough's commencement speech really hit home for me. While ideas are great, everybody has them, and so building a business is about so much more than the idea itself; it is all about the execution and the people you work with. Today really is just the beginning for you, so all that really matters is where you go from here. As you engage with the content in Part II, be sure you take the time to watch the commencement speech Jim Carrey gave to the 2014 graduating class of Maharishi University of Management – it's the best 26 minutes you'll spend on YouTube this week! Before reading the initial draft of this book, I hadn't heard the phrase "rejection therapy," but I'm incredibly glad it's covered here. You have to be able to sell to succeed, and that means you need to always be ready to make an ask knowing full well you may get rejected. Overcome your fear of rejection early on! Being rejected doesn't matter; I've been rejected so many times that it doesn't faze me anymore. I immediately turn around, make another pitch, and move on. Force yourself to be OK with rejection!

The book takes a turn in Part III. It's no longer about navigating your academic career or your individual mindset. It is now about the grit; the practical advice you need to succeed as a student entrepreneur. Here, Liguori talks about bolstering your sales acumen, and I can't emphasize enough how important it is you learn to sell. Greg Horn does a fantastic job of walking you through business accelerators, and the fact it's all grounded in his first-hand experience of being a student who took accelerator funding and went through the program to build a blitz crowdfunding platform really ties it all together. Who better could tell you about what to expect and consider. Last, I have to note the 70% rule (viz., "if you have 70% of the information, have done 70% of the analysis, and feel 70% confident, then move") is invaluable; I use it almost every day in almost every decision I make.

In sum, *The Startup Student* is a great read for any entrepreneur or any student but a must-read for every entrepreneurship student! But remember: You don't have to agree with everything in the book or even like every entry. Some stories will resonate with you more than others. That said, you won't find a better student-centric collection than what's in the pages that follow. Good luck, and I wish you nothing but success in your future!

–Steve

Preface

The idea for this book came about during a conversation with Daniel James Scott at Bar Louie Tampa in October of 2014. Daniel was just entering acquisition negotiations for his software startup and thinking of taking on a new challenge as Executive Director of the Tampa Bay Technology Forum. I was settling in at The University of Tampa after having spent the last three years at Fresno State's Lyles Center for Innovation and Entrepreneurship. From my recollection our conversation began with catching up on life and quickly transitioned to a discussion about the Tampa Bay Entrepreneurial Ecosystem, how it's changed over the last decade, what universities were doing well with regard to teaching entrepreneurship, and where there were gaps.

Right about this point in the conversation entered Kevin Moore. Kevin, a serial entrepreneur, had just moved to Tampa after leaving day-to-day operations of his company, Tier 1 Performance Solutions, as well as his long-time Entrepreneur-In-Residence position at Northern Kentucky University. His entry into the conversation was fortuitous, and the three of us spent the better part of an hour discussing the progress that still needed to be made in building appropriate curricula for the burgeoning field of entrepreneurship education.

During our discussion, we found ourselves spending quite a lot of time talking about the shortcomings of the texts used in many entrepreneurship courses. For example, many entrepreneurship textbooks teach students how to be entrepreneurs after graduation but fail to show them the best way to take advantage of the plethora of student-specific opportunities available to them while they're still in school. As we'll cover in later chapters, student entrepreneurs have certain distinct advantages over "real world" entrepreneurs, so failing to instruct students how to best take advantage of the leverage they've got going for them is doing them a major disservice.

To my surprise, Daniel and Kevin designated me as the person to tackle this problem, but I was less than enthused. The discussion continued a few more minutes and then we had our "A-ha!" moment: Any book that had any chance of meaningfully and impactfully instructing students on how to be successful entrepreneurship students and successful student entrepreneurs would have to contain input from a wide array of individuals with unique and varied backgrounds, experiences, and perspectives. At this point Kevin had to leave to attend another event. His departing words were "Eric, write that book," and I agreed to think it through.

It wasn't until the first part of 2015 that I was finally able to do the requisite soul searching that needed to happen before committing fully to this project. In the process, I revisited the work I'd done at the Lyles Center for Innovation and Entrepreneurship. Despite the Center's diverse programming, I'd always maintained a singular interest during my time there: helping university entrepreneurship students get the most out of their experience. Pursuing this passion led me in lots of different directions, including piloting a successful sales skills boot camp, developing a full sales skills workshop series for over 1,000 students, organizing Fresno State's first Startup Weekend, and infusing entrepreneurship into curricula across the university through our Entrepreneurship Ambassador Program (for which we took first place nationally, by the way). My team and I also sent a student to the Clinton Global Initiative summit, prepped students to pitch at the national level, and took our student community organizers to UP Summit where they met the likes of Brad Feld, Steve Case, Mary Grove, and dozens of other incredible entrepreneurial thought leaders.

Let's now hop across the Atlantic Ocean to Mikkeli, Finland where I was teaching a course on innovation in the global economy. Late one evening after class, I finally put pen to paper and wrote a draft solicitation letter and scope for the book project and sent it to Daniel for review. He wrote back with feedback almost instantly, thrilled to see me moving forward – probably because it meant he didn't have to do it himself, but I won't hold that against him – but also pointing out that I still didn't have any type of validation that there was a need for such an effort. (We didn't doubt the need existed for one moment, but Daniel rightfully figured that a use case or two would be helpful in outlining the project more clearly.)

The next day after class, a student approached me to ask if I'd be willing to talk with some friends of his who were working on a new tech venture. My time in Mikkeli was nearing an end, but I agreed to meet them the next night at 7pm anyway. When the time came for me to leave for the meeting, the below-freezing weather and pitch-black Finnish night completely zapped any enthusiasm I had for leaving my warm and well-lit apartment, but nevertheless I made the trek to Parnell's Pub to meet Bruno Jacobsen and Markus Kurjonen for the first time.

Time flew by as Bruno, Markus, and I spoke for over three hours about how they could maximize the opportunities available to them as students. As these types of conversations tend to do, our discussion ended with far more thanks for my time than were necessary, a request to meet again the next night if possible, and Bruno asking for my help in two specific ways: (1) helping them figure out how to better present themselves and their idea in the future and (2) putting together a list of resources that related to the advice I'd given them during the course of the evening. I agreed to both points.

The next morning, I received this email from Bruno (and a similar one from Markus, too):

> Hey, professor.
>
> Just wanted to thank you for yesterday. It was a pretty cool evening…you gave us a lot of valuable advice and information. I'm looking forward to seeing you tonight again. Have fun in Helsinki!
>
> BR,
> Bruno

Before our follow-up meeting later that night, I did some research on who they were and what information was out there on them and their idea. I also spent some time brainstorming opportunities specific to students that they could leverage so I could offer them some definitive options and advice. We met again for two hours, and then it was time to part ways as it was my last night in Mikkeli. The next day I received another email from Bruno (and, again, a similar one from Markus):

> Hi, Eric!
>
> Thanks for everything yesterday. We really appreciate it. We could scarcely believe you'd take so much of your busy time to help us out.
>
> This is really good stuff and we'll look into all of this. I'll get

together with Mark and look at everything we can do and possible people we want to connect with as you suggested.

I hope we can find a way to be of some value to you as well, either now or in the future. And if there is anything I can help with, please let me know, too. It's my pleasure.

We'll stay in touch.

Bruno

Needless to say, without looking, I had found preliminary validation there was a need for a book covering exactly the type of information included here: practical advice for you, the student entrepreneur, on how to make (and get) the most out of your educational and entrepreneurial experience. In reflecting back over the last few years, a few other students very similar to Bruno and Markus have taken some of the very content in this book to heart and achieved success. As you read on, you'll hear their stories and learn exactly what they did, why they did it, and how things turned out. In the process, you'll also get tons of insight and even some candid advice from top entrepreneurs and a few faculty as well, all of which will help you maximize your odds of success.

Introduction

One of the fastest growing majors on college campuses across the nation, entrepreneurship has earned a reputation as a valuable yet hard-to-classify area of study that often crosses disciplinary borders. While most universities house entrepreneurship in the business school, doing so is not a hard and fast rule: Stanford's program is under an engineering umbrella, Oklahoma State University established a freestanding School of Entrepreneurship in 2008, and in December 2015 Florida State announced a $100 million gift to create what will soon be the largest interdisciplinary school of entrepreneurship in the nation.

Some would argue these are extreme examples and that there is no real traction in entrepreneurship education, but that's factually incorrect. There are over 5,000 entrepreneurship courses offered annually at over 2,000 U.S. colleges and universities alone, and global data shows there are more college students and recent graduates starting businesses than ever before, with *The Global Entrepreneurship Monitor* estimating there are 135 million early stage entrepreneurs age 18 to 25. Moreover, appreciation for entrepreneurship education is not limited to higher education. Much like their collegiate counterparts, many high school administrators are beginning to recognize the inherent value in instilling an entrepreneurial spirit in their students. For instance, Connor Alstrom, Lynn Kroesen, and I successfully piloted an Entrepreneurial Leadership Academy for high school students in Florida in the summer of 2015, and in the fall of 2015 the Fresno Unified School District opened the Philip J. Patiño School of Entrepreneurship, which will serve up to 450 10th through 12th grade students annually over the next two and a half years.

This book, *The Startup Student*, emerged from the demonstrated growth in demand for entrepreneurship education. Divided into three separate yet related parts, it is designed to be a resource, a tool, a reference guide, and a source of wisdom for all those brave student souls willing to put their ideas into action in entrepreneurship classrooms around the world.

Part 1, Succeeding as an Entrepreneurship Student, offers students advice on how to successfully navigate an entrepreneurship program, touching on topics such as acquiring startup internships, dealing with faculty, avoiding common idea generation pitfalls, and getting the most out of one's entrepreneurship education. Part 2, Bolstering Your Entrepreneurial Mindset, discusses key psychological factors needed for entrepreneurial success. Meanwhile, Part 3, Succeeding as a Student Entrepreneur, draws upon the advice of a variety of experienced entrepreneurs and new venture experts to give students the tips they need to launch a startup while still in school.

It is important to note that there is no right or wrong way to read this book. Jump around, start with Part 2, take it in over time in many small doses, or devour it cover-to-cover in a single afternoon – the choice is yours. No matter your decision, know that each of the book's contributors offered advice in their own words and personality, the sum of which is an anthology chock-full of a variety of writing styles, refreshing candor, and valuable words of wisdom. After several of the entries, and outlined in black boxes, are my personal thoughts to accompany the entry; these words are my own and not the work of the individual authors.

I hope that you not only enjoy The Startup Student, but that you walk away feeling enriched and inspired by it as well. As you dive into the entries that follow, I suspect you will find a lot of information you can use both immediately and as you move further down the path of launching your venture. As I tell my own entrepreneurship students at the end of each semester, good luck and stay in touch. You can reach me at info@ thestartupstudent.co – I'd love to know what you are working on and how I can help.

Part 1

Succeeding as an Entrepreneurship Student

"If you don't know it's impossible it's easier to do. And because nobody's done it before, they haven't made up rules to stop anyone doing that again yet."

– Neil Gaiman
Carnegie Medal-Winning Author

Ignore Faculty Opinions
Doan Winkel

Faculty have a lot to say. They love to pontificate. In class, they lecture way too much. Outside class, they likely don't give you concise answers. You will hear way too many opinions as you progress through your entrepreneurship journey. In too many classes, without you asking, faculty will offer their opinion on any variety of startup topics.

My advice (as one of those educators). . . ignore faculty opinions.

That's right. Their opinions are nearly worthless. Too often, entrepreneurship faculty have never been entrepreneurs themselves, or if they have been, it was long ago. And those rare faculty who are true entrepreneurs usually don't stick around in academia very long because they can't stand to work within that sort of bureaucracy. In any case, faculty opinions will likely be based on either anecdotal evidence or academic research that's disconnected from the real world, and following those sort of well-intentioned but ill-informed opinions will only lead you into wasting resources – death for a startup.

I have a hard time finding much value in the opinions of most faculty because what you ultimately need to know is (1) what to do next and (2) how to do it. You need forward-looking provocation when all many faculty can offer is backward-looking reflection. Reflection can be valuable in many settings, but not when it comes to advice for you on your startup. Furthermore, if faculty actually do come up with good opinions, they likely lack the context in which to apply the opinion they're sharing. That lack of implementation is considerably dangerous. Do you want opinions that will help you progress along your entrepreneurial process? Talk to entrepreneurs – those who are in the real world executing daily, falling down, getting up, and going all in.

Connect, Connect, Connect

If you ignore their opinions, then what value can faculty offer you? For faculty who give a damn about their students, they can offer really valuable connections. Often faculty (especially entrepreneurship faculty) will have extensive local networks of entrepreneurs, business leaders, and investors. Use them for that. I have started a few companies and am in the process of launching a few more. While I have opinions about how to most effectively go about launching and running a business, I find that I create the greatest value for my students through connecting them with mentors, champions, and provocateurs.

Community members are extremely interested in what students are doing and in giving back to help students succeed, but they often have a very difficult time finding ways to meaningfully contribute to students' development. Find faculty who are engaging community members in novel and deliberate ways – not just as guest speakers, but in workshops, in events, in panel discussions, and in student organizations. Those faculty understand the power of building relationships. Get to know those faculty members – stop by their office hours, invite them to coffee, talk to them about your ideas and aspirations. They will help you by connecting you with the right people, and such connections are so much more valuable than unfounded or outdated opinions.

Filling Up Your Toolbox

In addition to deep and meaningful networks, faculty have tremendous tools at their disposal. One thing we faculty do really well (for the most part) is research. In figuring out how to teach entrepreneurship, most faculty will have thoroughly investigated the variety of tools available – from the business plan to the Business Model Canvas to proforma templates to NDA, IP, and other legal documents. Maybe you're preparing to search out angel investors for investment. Maybe you need to do some user testing. Maybe you need to build a cash flow projection. Ask the faculty for the appropriate tool(s) to accomplish your next goal, and they will share the tools with you. They will also share opinions about things you should or should not be doing. Don't listen!

As a faculty member myself, I have lots of tools at my disposal. I will listen to my students talk about their obstacles and suggest a tool or two that might help. I don't do much explaining about why I chose that tool or how I think they should use it. You're an adult; you need to take ownership of your experiences and figure out your own answers. Giving you my opinions doesn't provide value to you – the value is created by me listening, providing tools, and pushing you to answer your own questions.

We're Not All Bad

Most faculty have good intentions. We want to help our students. We spend countless hours outside class meeting with students, helping with projects, and connecting students with others in our network. We bring a ton of resources to our students, and we are very ready to share those resources with the students who put in the effort to stand out somehow. The most dangerous resource we have, however, is our opinion. Take advantage of our network. Take advantage of the tools we have at our disposal. Take advantage of our willingness to help. But please, please, for the sake of your startup's survival, ignore our opinions. At the end of the day the only opinions that matter are those of your customers – listen to them very closely, and ignore all the other noise.

> I asked Doan to write about ignoring faculty opinions because he's a boat-rocker who I could trust to be candid with you. I chose his entry as the first entry in the book to remind you to take everything you read here, and everything you encounter in your classes, with a grain of salt. That said, there's a lot of wisdom in Doan's words. Brad Feld and David Cohen, authors of *Do More Faster*, talk about how startups get input from a variety of sources, noting that often this input is contradictory. At the end of the day, you are the one who has to live with the outcomes of the decisions you make, so you need to decide who to listen to and how much to listen to them. Remember: We're often operating with imperfect and incomplete information, and despite what some mystics may tell you, nobody is clairvoyant.

"Everyone who's ever taken a shower has had an idea. It's the person who gets out of the shower, dries off and does something about it who makes a difference."

– Nolan Bushnell
Founder of Atari, Inc.

Coming Up With an Idea - Avoid the Obvious Paths
Eric Liguori

Every semester a fresh crop of students undergoes the same exercises in entrepreneurship classrooms across the country. They're told to come up with new venture ideas by journaling their daily frustrations. After a week or so of journaling, they're told to generate a "bug report," or a bulleted report of everything that bugged them over the past week, and develop solutions to solve the problems.

Having watched this cycle repeat itself many times, I now know that each group of students, no matter how unique, will inevitably report having the same few pain points as the students that came before them. And if you've ever taken an entrepreneurship class, you've probably even thought of some of them yourself.

1. Laundry Services: Thinking of a campus laundry service or laundry delivery service? You're not alone. The universal dislike of doing laundry plus the inconvenience of dormitory life makes for a pretty logical pain point for many college students around the globe.

2. Alcohol / Meal / Coffee Delivery Services: Yes, it sucks to be at a party, run out of drinks, and not be able to drive safely to get more. Yes, it also sucks later that same night when you need some food and can't go get it. And yes, it sucks when you oversleep the next day, have to rush to class, and are dying for that cup of coffee you did not have time to pick up. Many of you would welcome a solution to these problems that allowed for (a) a fresh bottle of Bacardi to arrive at midnight when the party is really taking off, (b) a Taco Bell nightcap to roll in around three in the morning, and (c) a piping hot Starbucks latte waiting for you on Monday morning as you're rushing to make it to class on time.

3. Parking: At this point I think I've heard every potential solution to campus and downtown parking situations known to man, including variations local to Louisiana, California, Florida, and even Finland. One semester brought forth balloon-like devices that would rise above open parking spaces to make them visible, while another semester dreamed up weight-sensing plates that could detect a vehicle's presence in a space and change an indicator light from green to red. On other occasions the solution du jour was a mobile app that kept track of all available parking spots.

All of the above ideas offer solutions to the identified pain points. The problem is that the solutions are either not easily implemented (e.g., students propose an app but cannot build it) or are simply too expensive. So despite semesters upon semesters of bug report exercises yielding nearly identical results, students still do their own laundry, pick up their own coffee, and find their own parking spots.

There must be a problem in the process, right? How else could it be that the same universal problems continue to persist despite countless entrepreneurship students across the globe working to solve them? The answer lies in the fact that the students' ideas are often evaluated on the basis of radicalism instead of reality, causing them to forgo small-scale yet practical solutions in favor of flashy options that can realistically never be brought to fruition.

Below are a few steps you can follow to avoid wasting precious time pursuing an unattainable idea.

Is the problem you've identified the real problem?

Doan Winkel and Michael Luchies host a podcast called *Trepidemic*. In episode three, Doan talks about how every semester a group of his students will wish to create an alcohol delivery service (see, I told you!) yet pay no attention to the legal, financial, and bureaucratic implications of their proposed solution. As Doan says in the podcast,

> It's easy to come up with solutions. Making them good, viable business opportunities is what's difficult. The common denominator here is to back up and say, 'OK, alcohol delivery is a great solution to the problem you specified, but is the problem you specified really the problem?' If you get inside the head of the drunk college student who's running out of alcohol, perhaps the problem has less to do with them wanting more alcohol to drink and more to do with them not wanting to have people leave because they ran out of alcohol. They don't want the party to stop – that's your real problem, and perhaps there is an alternate solution to this problem that

avoids all the legal and insurance hurdles that make alcohol delivery unviable in many localities.

Is your solution BOLD?

Be bold in everything you do. Have the guts to think big and believe you can conquer the world. Question the status quo. Take the time to get to know yourself and what matters most to you, then commit to doing it. As Mahatma Gandhi said, "Action expresses priorities."

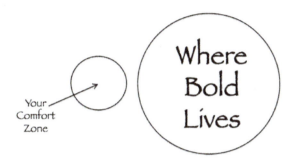

Boldness is requisite when seeking new ideas. Big challenges require big solutions, and bold ideas should, almost by definition, be outside of your comfort zone. So think big and seek massively scalable solutions to real problems without worrying about how disruptive they may be.

The introduction of Uber into the transportation marketplace upset the entire industry, landing the company the #1 spot on *VentureBeat*'s December 2014 Naughty and Nice list. Uber's valuation that same month was estimated at $41 billion. According to Y-Combinator's Paul Graham, naughtiness is a desired trait for startup founders, so don't let trivial barriers stop you from identifying fearless solutions. Be like Uber and be bold.

For the record, I'm not bashing any of the ideas mentioned here. At one point, I had a "no t-shirt company" rule for my students. I ended up dropping that rule after a former student of mine at Fresno State closed $50,000+ worth of custom shirt preorders in a three-week period of time. Focus less on any specific example here and more on the "be bold" mantra.

The finalist pitches for the prestigious million-dollar Hult Prize are a prime example of how bold thinking can pay off in spades. The 2015 competition began with over 60,000 students around the globe working toward one objective: "Build sustainable and scalable social enterprises to address early childhood education in urban slums and beyond." One of our University of Tampa (UT) teams, Team Tembo (pictured below with President Clinton), made it to the final round, which put them in the top six globally. How? Tembo, as well as the other five finalist teams, came up with a bold solution to a global problem.

Pictured from left to right: Brent Caramanica, Phil Michaels, President Clinton, Sercan Topcu, Ulixes Hawili.

"The answer to success: Be smart, daring, and different."

– Ron Klein
"The Grandfather of Possibilities"

Live The Gift
Evan English Ernst

In 2012, while I was a junior at Florida State, I brought together a group of my best friends in room 114 of Phi Kappa Tau to ask a simple, yet colossal question: Could we create a national movement to protect the hearts of student athletes?

Outside of being born and raised in Cocoa Beach, FL, my friends and I all had one thing in common: the death of our lifelong teammate, Rafe Maccarone, due to a detectable heart condition while at soccer practice. Here's what we knew: Our story represented a preventable tragedy faced by thousands of teams, families, and communities across the country annually. Here's what we didn't know: everything else.

Back in room 114, we weren't sure if creating a nonprofit was the best approach to answering our question, and the last thing we wanted to do was to start a nonprofit just to say we did it. To avoid reinventing the wheel, we called every organization in the country with a mission similar to ours, and from those phone calls we confirmed our hypothesis: A major void existed in protecting the hearts of student athletes across the country. With the vision of honoring the life of our fallen teammate and putting an end to preventable tragedies, we created Who We Play For. Tragedy to trajectory, we said.

Right out of the gate, we struggled with mission creep. We donated AEDs, we gave out scholarships, we provided CPR training, and we advocated for legislation. We had a ton of support from our community, and we wanted to do it all. Fortunately for us, after driving all night to Washington, D.C. to meet with nonprofit guru Mark Shriver, we were finally able to pinpoint our purpose: solve the biggest public health problem in athletics, sudden cardiac arrest, by providing electrocardiogram (EKG) heart screenings.

It's the greatest privilege of my life to say that Who We Play For has now screened over 70,000 young hearts and, in the process, detected over 60 undiagnosed life-threatening heart conditions in student-athletes. In addition, we successfully lobbied to require sudden cardiac arrest education, we provided the first heart screening in a developing country, we created the first network of college chapters to protect the hearts of student-athletes, and we inspired a book titled *Bliss*. Below are the three biggest pieces of the puzzle that enabled us to turn a question into one of the biggest heart screening non-profits in the world.

#1. Do it for the eulogy

If you're reading this book and you're a student entrepreneur, I can almost guarantee I know your biggest problem. You either have a couple ideas and you're not sure which one to choose, or you're already working on two or more ideas. In my humble opinion, I think the most common mistake made by my fellow student entrepreneurs is juggling multiple startups. Everyone seems to think they're the outlier that can make it work amid their limited resources and busy schedules, including me. Hubris, unfortunately, is real.

When faced with the challenge of knowing which path to choose, I recommend writing out exactly why you want to pursue each startup. Fight the temptation to pick the most lucrative option, and instead go all in on the idea that best encompasses your passion. When the day comes for the people you love most to deliver your eulogy, which startup will you want to define you?

#2. "I am not an expert"

The most important five words I've said on this journey have been "I am not an expert." While recognizing our strengths has been valuable, understanding our weaknesses and knowing when to ask for help have been far more critical to our success. Our ability to be authentic and transparent and own that we're the farthest thing from experts in just about everything has provided us a way past every roadblock. Our team is not a team of doctors with formal medical training, nor is it a team of trained emergency medical technicians. Instead, we are a team of people who are willing to do whatever necessary – including seeking outside help – to solve the problem at hand.

#3. Live the gift

Starting a student-led company will be extremely demanding and gratifying and come with its share of ups and downs. Personally and professionally,

I believe perspective on the journey is everything. Perspective is where positivity starts and hope replenishes. If there's one thing I've learned, it's that not everyone is fortunate enough to have the same opportunities that you have as a student and as an entrepreneur. Starting a company is a privilege and a gift. My challenge to you is simple: Live the gift.

I first met Evan and learned about Who We Play For in January of 2015 when I moderated a panel discussion at the annual meeting of the United States Association for Small Business and Entrepreneurship. Evan was one of the student panelists chosen to participate based on a stellar nomination from his mentors at Florida State University. The passion and dedication to mission of Evan and the entire Who We Play For team immediately impressed me upon our first meeting. They're traveling the country saving lives, one school or team at a time. This photo shows Evan and some of the Who We Play For Team right after finishing a heart screening at Merritt Island High School.

"You get 10 doors slammed in your face. The secret is to show up at door #11 just as enthusiastic as you were at door #1."

– John Paul DeJoria
Co-Founder, House of Blues and The Patron Spirits Company

Exploiting Networks
Eric Liguori

Most students don't think they have a large and meaningful network to exploit, but they're usually wrong. Are you connected to friends on Facebook, Twitter, Instagram, and/or LinkedIn? That's your network. Yet, unfortunately many networks often go unnoticed or unexplored for two reasons:

1. Most adults, and especially students, don't view their current networks as resources to be exploited, and

2. They often don't realize or drastically underestimate the ability of a network to snowball into something massive.

Topher Morrison, founding partner of KPI USA, uses a great analogy to illustrate the inherent value that lies in networks: Think of your networks as a tree, with all of your direct contacts forming the trunk. Then, think of your contacts' contacts (viz., your 2nd degree connections) as branches and your contacts' contacts' contacts (viz., your 3rd degree connections) as the fruit coming off the branches. The majority of value in your network lies in the fruit of your tree, not the trunk. The challenge lies in maneuvering up the trunk, across the branches, and down to the fruit.

As a student, there are several things you can do right on campus to populate your trunk and begin your quest for fruit. By default you are part of a university network of professors, administrators, and staff, many of whom you interact with on a daily or weekly basis. These folks are your trunk; take the time to get to know them, connect with them on LinkedIn, and build a professional relationship. By nature of the assortment of disciplines on every college campus, you instantly have access to a diverse group of people from whom you can begin branching out your tree.

The networks that surround universities and faculty are enormous, and the reach they have is much greater than you realize. If your goal is to find opportunities for exploitation, then you should be jumping at the chance to harness the human capital you're surrounded by each day. Here are two methods my former students have used to maximize their networks, and I guarantee you'll be able to accomplish the same if you put forth the effort.

#1: Blindly asking someone if they "know anyone who can help you" is a path to nowhere: Do the legwork for them and make a specific ask!

So you have a problem and are in search of a solution (e.g., you need some subject matter expertise, you need to find a co-founder, or you need an internship). You are a well-intentioned student, you work hard, and you have a respectable GPA. Having read the paragraphs above you decide to start asking the individuals in your campus network if they know anyone who can help you. Being good-natured and generally helpful people, they try and maybe make an introduction or two, but ultimately you get nowhere.

In this example, you failed because you did not do any work to help your connection help you and because you were not specific enough in your ask. An exponentially better approach involves being proactive and being specific, both necessary characteristics for exploiting a network where the majority of value lies in 3rd degree connections. First, take the time to fully identify and articulate what it is you want. Consider what happened to Bobby, a current student of mine, during a recent Q&A session with one of my guest speakers for the semester. The conversation went like this:

- Bobby: What advice would you have for me on how to get an internship?
- Speaker: You need to be much more specific. What type of internship are you looking for?
- Bobby: I'm looking for an opportunity to gain some experience.
- Speaker: OK, but experience in what? What's your major? What are you interested in?
- Bobby: I am a finance major with a marketing minor, but I'm very personable and a hard worker and think I could add value to a business in any department.
- Speaker: But what industry do you want to work in? What interests you? What are your passionate about?
- Bobby: I really like sports. Ultimately I want to get into sports finance, so if I could find an opportunity there it'd be ideal.
- Speaker: Now we're where we need to be! You're specific. I can connect you with my buddy, John, who is a sports agent and negotiates contracts for sports athletes. He's hired interns in the past so maybe he knows of an opportunity.

This dialogue was painful to watch unfold, and it played out exactly the same way in my head as I was thinking of how I could help Bobby with his problem. Bobby simply took too long to provide the specific information needed for us to help him make a valuable connection. When he first asked the question, I drew a blank on who I'd connect him with and defaulted to referring him to our internship office. Then, when Bobby said finance, my mind went to connecting him with my brother who is a manager at a pretty large national bank. But when Bobby finally said sports finance, the bells went off. I know someone who manages finances for over 140 professional athletes and who has a track record of being willing to talk to students and hire interns.

Unfortunately, most people, faculty included, have neither the time nor patience to wait to get the information they need to help make useful connections. Faculty are busy and constantly bombarded with requests like Bobby's, so they don't want to have go on a fact-finding mission to learn what they need to know. And, frankly, they shouldn't have to; that burden falls on the individual asking for help.

Limited time and patience aren't the only reasons to be specific and proactive, however. You'll also deal with the fact that it is difficult for many people to keep tabs on their networks. For example, it is not feasible for me to be expected to keep up with the 1,000+ people I am connected with on LinkedIn. Frankly, even if I had the time, I'm not smart enough to remember where each of them worked, what they did there, what industry it was in, what their interests are, what education they have, etc. So, if you want me to help you in the best way possible, you need to do the legwork for me. Get on LinkedIn and search my network by keyword for the type of help you are seeking, then bring me a list of my relevant connections and ask me for an introduction.

I had a great student a few years back, Greg, who can attest to the power of this approach in helping uncover hidden gems. Greg owned several bowling alley pro shops and was constantly looking for ways to internalize production to achieve higher margins (e.g., mixing his own bowling ball cleaning solution and bottling it for sale). For his class project, Greg was looking for a way to polish bowling balls without clogging the pores in the polyurethane resin material that covers them. He spent a lot of time experimenting and researching potential solutions to no avail since he wasn't a chemist or a materials scientist.

Greg, taking our classroom discussion of specificity and legwork to heart, searched through my LinkedIn network for people who could help him. He found the chair of our Chemistry Department and asked me to send an email on his behalf. The chair, in turn, emailed some of his colleagues at other universities, and to mine and Greg's surprise, we got the following response from a faculty member a few hours north of us: "I'd be glad to talk with your student. Prior to coming back into academia a few years ago, I was a urethane scientist at 3M for 10 years and this sounds like an interesting project."

In just a few days time, Greg hopped on the phone with this guy, and it turned out to be a perfect match. This kind faculty member spent several hours helping Greg explore options and feasibility and never charged him a dime for his help. Ultimately, Greg chose to abandon the project for feasibility reasons (R&D costs outweighed reasonable profitability estimates) and because a new opportunity popped up that caused Greg to pivot (it was a very profitable pivot, so all is well).

#2: Work smarter, not harder: Target those with the most fruit to offer first.

Some individuals on college campuses have more expansive networks than others. While network size is sometimes a function of personality, it can also be influenced by the individual's role on campus. Junior faculty at many research-oriented campuses, for example, are told to keep their heads down and focus primarily on research, a lifestyle that doesn't particularly lend itself to building large, productive networks. That said, many people in and around your campus are in positions where building meaningful relationships with the business and entrepreneurial community is a core function of their jobs. These folks are the ones I suggest you begin with if your goal is to build out a resource-dense network. Of course, don't totally ignore the junior faculty, but know they may not be the best place to start.

To help you get started, I've put together a list of the three categories of people my students have found to be the most fruitful campus super-connectors: the money raisers, the movers and shakers, and the administrators.

The Money Raisers

Almost every university has a team of fundraising staff who spend the majority of their time keeping in touch with alumni and the business community. They facilitate positive relationships with local businesspeople, let alumni and donors know how they can give back to the university, and help keep interested parties aware of all the exciting developments and student accomplishments happening on campus. Given that these folks' jobs revolve around nurturing connections, it is not surprising that they typically have very large networks filled with lots of meaningful connections.

My experience has been that fund development professionals love it when respectful students are willing to take the time to accompany them on meetings with potential donors or friends of the university to help tell the story of the university firsthand. Finding fund development professionals' contact info should be as simple as looking for it on your university website. Send them an email and ask to stop by and talk to them for a few minutes. Introduce yourself. Show them this article. See if they can help get you involved. To get them on your side, you'll certainly have to agree to play ball and follow their rules, which include first and foremost that you won't solicit startup capital from anyone you meet with them. You can find capital elsewhere; instead, use this as an opportunity to make a good connection with an established businessperson who can help you build out your core network in the future.

The Movers and Shakers

The professionals running the centers and institutes at your university tend to be well-known both in the community and in the industry on which their center or institute is focused. Their research gets exposure, the media contacts them for expert advice, and their events bring the public onto campus. Take the time to volunteer a few hours in their offices or at their big events to get to know them better. They can make introductions for you and will perhaps even let you pass out promotional materials for your startup at their next event or tell you where to send your big press release. It would be silly to not get to know these professionals a bit better as they can offer experience, good will, and network connections all at once.

The Administrators

For some crazy reason many students don't ever try to get to know the administrators running the university they are paying a ton of money to attend. When I ask why this is, most students usually cite indifference or fear, neither of which makes much sense. The deans, provosts, and presidents of your university are generally kind, student-focused leaders working day in and day out to ensure you have a good college experience. They likely got into academia because they were passionate about teaching and seeing students succeed, even if they now spend most of their time managing the business of the university.

I'd be willing to bet if you sent an email to your dean, provost, and/or president asking for a ten-minute meeting to make introductions, at least one of them, if not all three, would schedule some time with you. Try it and see what happens. If you're successful, schedule the meeting, introduce yourself, and let them know about your aspirations and passions. Once you get home, connect with them on LinkedIn, search their networks, and ask them for specific introductions. The worst thing they can say is no, and if they do, consider it rejection therapy. It's good for the soul.

Two UT undergraduate students, Chantalle Blundell (left) and Brittany Blonder (right) got to meet serial entrepreneur Ron Klein (center) via a networking connection from a class speaker. Klein patented the magnetic strip on the back of credit cards and developed the first up to the minute bond quotation and trade information system for the New York Stock Exchange.

"Stay hungry. Stay foolish."

– Stewart Brand
Editor, *Whole Earth Catalog*

(the quote that inspired Steve Jobs)

Playing the Student Card

Birton Cowden

Many have the perception that entrepreneurship is a "grown-up" sport. Sure, there is a stigma associated with being a student: "adults" in the "real world" envision "poor college students" trying to survive on ramen and the occasional cheap beer. This stigma comes with some perks, however, as often the very same "adults" that brand you as poor also want to help you in any way that they can. In fact, at this very moment, a growing number of initiatives exist solely to assist you, college student and the future of our economy, in becoming a job creator for yourself and others.

Congratulations! You're in the sweet spot for getting valuable free stuff to start a company. In today's economy, playing the entrepreneurship student card is your VIP access pass to otherwise expensive resources in the form of capital, individual expertise, services, and tools. Here's some more information about what's available to you and how you can get it for yourself.

Free Money

Almost every university has a pool of donations to give to students interested in starting their own venture, and in the rare chance that such a pool does not exist, there are typically local foundations or institutes than give grant money to student entrepreneurs. So the money's there if you're willing to find it. Even better, there are typically no strings attached to the money – all you have to do is fill out an application or get a nomination from a professor. For instance, the Harold Grinspoon Foundation in western Massachusetts has an entrepreneurial initiative dedicated to giving a few hundred dollars to students who demonstrate entrepreneurial spirit. From just these small sums of money, many students have been able to do market tests of their ideas, including one student who used his prize money to buy a sock printing press and 100 pairs of black socks and is now selling over 5,000 pairs of socks per month.

In addition, you may have heard that many ventures get their initial funding from the three F's: friends, family, and fools. As mentioned above, there is a common misperception that all college students are poor, so why not use it to your advantage? Share your ideas with everyone with whom you come into contact, and there's a good chance at least one of the three F's will be feeling generous. And unlike online crowd-sourcing platforms like Kickstarter, all these donors want in return is to see you do something awesome.

Free Time

As with money, people are also willing to donate their time to help college students be successful. Mentors are important for every aspect of life. While you may not have the most extensive network, you do have a common bond with the thousands of individuals that are alumni of your school. In the entire network of the university, there has to be at least one expert in your field that can help you get to the next level, including giving you access to high-profile entrepreneurs. For example, Indiana University students could find a connection to Indiana alumnus Mark Cuban, and U Mass undergrads may know someone who knows someone who knows Wayne Chang (Dropbox and Crashlytics co-founder) or Jeff Taylor (Monster.com founder). Every school has successful alumni, and your connection to them is a lot closer than you may think. Do not underestimate the power of the alumni bond.

You can also play your student card to gather data for customer development. Doing customer interviews can be a daunting task, as it is hard to get people to take the time to talk with you. As a student, however, you have a magic phrase that tugs at the heartstrings of potential interviewees: "Can I interview you for a class project I'm working on?" After hearing this, you'll find people are willing to sit with you longer and give you more feedback than they would have otherwise, thus making your data more accurate while helping establish a new relationship with a potential mentor or future customer.

Free Stuff

Getting free stuff is another perk of being an entrepreneurship student. Many companies like Amazon, Microsoft, and Google offer students free access to tools as part of their participation in hackathons or other programs. In addition, many software vendors make free or discounted licenses available for educational purposes. And remember, if a vendor does not claim a discount on their website, it never hurts to call them and play the student card. You represent a juicy target market to many vendors. Because of your potential to be an early adopter on your campus and a paying customer in the future, these vendors might offer you free access or an extended demo.

You can also access lots of free or discounted resources through your university. Whether a graphic designer, a mechanical engineer, or an architect, you can probably find at least one computer on campus loaded with the software you need. Additionally, make sure to scope out everything available to you through your school's library, as many libraries have access to extensive online databases and lots of other little-known perks. And finally, check to see if your university has a relationship with a law firm willing to do pro bono or discounted work for students. A program like this can help you file a patent or get the licenses you need at a fraction of the cost.

Lots of good stuff, right? Free resources like those listed here are sitting around waiting for student entrepreneurs to claim them, so get at it before you enter the "real world" and it's too late. Do your research and talk with your entrepreneurial allies (your university's center for entrepreneurship, the local SBDC, local economic councils, etc.) to find out everything that's within your reach, and then get out there and stake your claim to create a competitive advantage for your new venture.

The student card is one of the most valuable tools in your arsenal, and it immediately disappears when you graduate. I recently took a group of students to a local business to talk to a serial entrepreneur. While I'll keep things anonymous for obvious reasons, he told the class that when he and his partner launched their flagship business, he "absolutely lied to vendors and competitors" he wanted to get information from by "telling them or leading them to believe" he was still a student. He said he found he got a much different and more receptive response to people by playing the student card.

For a quick, project-based intern that won't cost you too much, check out www.internrocket.com. (It's also a great site to use if you're looking for micro-internships yourself. They provide short internship experiences to help existing companies and startups alike find paid student talent for micro-projects.)

"You can fail at what you don't want, so you might as well take a chance at doing what you love."

– Jim Carrey
Golden Globe-Winning Actor / Comedian

Startup Internships
Josh Bendickson & Eric Liguori

As a student your time is always tight. You have multiple courses taking up your time with lectures, homework, and studying, and you probably also have a job that, perhaps out of necessity, demands a good portion of your days. And of course your social life takes time as well – it's only healthy to have some work-life balance, right? So as a good student, you manage your schedule wisely and try to achieve some form of equilibrium. You sacrifice your social life during exam week, sometimes take an extra class to get ahead, and perhaps consider enrolling in summer courses to lighten your load during the fall and spring semesters.

Conventional wisdom as well as most faculty, parents, and advisors suggest you complete an internship or two while enrolled in college to make your resume more impressive to future employers. They contend it will enable you to better understand "business" and how "business" really works. They cite countless valid stories of past individuals who turned internships into jobs. You can't argue with the logic; internships are highly practical and valuable experiences. Internships at startups, however, are made from a different mold. Whereas an internship with a Big Four accounting firm comes with a defined conversion rate to full time employment and major name recognition on the resume, internships at startups carry the stigma of free labor.

I don't think startup internships are bad. Well, let me restate that: I don't think all startup internships are bad, and I think some offer the best of all possible experiences. Brian McKearney graduated from North Carolina State University in December 2011. While he was a student at NC State, he completed three internships: one with an angel investment firm, one with The Walt Disney Company, and one with a startup called Avancen. Avancen (www.avancen.com) created the first FDA-approved device to administer patient-controlled delivery of oral pain medication. Here is what Brian had to say about his experience:

> Interning with a startup is unlike any job opportunity you will ever have. Your job description and general role are fuzzy at best. But then yet so is every position within a startup. Everyone has to wear every single hat otherwise the company would buckle.

I learned more in that one summer about how companies operate, how to sell, accounting, product development, and many more topics than many of my contemporaries have now learned in the four years since graduating college and holding full-time corporate jobs.

What I learned, and the experience I gained, fanned the flame of the entrepreneurial spark I knew was always inside of me. It is what led me to start two different companies after I graduated. Toward the end of the life cycle of the second company, I knew I did not want to go at it alone again, but also that I was just not fit for corporate America. As such I called up my old boss who I had kept in touch with over the years. Unlike a contact in a large company, he was actually able to help me on the spot. He had an opening, and based on a relationship that we formed from working so closely together one summer, he offered me the position right then and there.

Brian is now Avancen's director of business development, a role in which he is intimately involved in developing distribution agreements, forming strategic partnerships, and raising an $11 million B round of funding. More importantly, Brian's experience interning for a startup is not uncommon. Collin Steinmetz joined ilumi as a sales and marketing intern two months after graduating from the University of Texas at Dallas. In a recent email exchange, Collin mentioned that "working at a startup can be hectic and stressful, but this comes with the territory of gaining real-world experience in several different aspects of the industry at the same time." Interns in conventional internship programs commonly are exposed to only one functional department (e.g., marketing) within a single industry (e.g., financial services). Good startup internships push interns to work much more cross-functionally, often spanning several departments and industries. Collin embraced the challenge and was hired full time in ilumi's sales and marketing department after only three months as an intern.

Let's also look at this from the startup's perspective. Claire Jones owns The General Store Seattle (www.thegeneralstoreseattle.com), which she started in early 2015. Recently Claire began using interns to help grow her startup. Claire notes:

The fundamental difference between working for an established company versus a startup is that we as a company are still forming and establishing business practices and protocol. This involves defining day-to-day, week-to-week, month-to-month, quarter-to-quarter, and year-to-year tasks. It is important to make year-long projections and objectives to systematize a business so that it can run (and succeed) without relying on one single employee/worker. The biggest potential for personal growth lies in the ability and willingness to ask, "Can this be done in a better, more efficient way?

Interns in startups have the unique opportunity to actually take part in shaping a business from the ground up. They get the unique chance to help form these protocols.

There are many factors to consider when evaluating startup internship opportunities. The list below outlines a few things to do as you consider whether or not to take an internship in a startup (or any internship, really):

1. Vet the founders. Ask about their backgrounds, prior successes and failures, level of education, etc. Collin knew the risks of taking an internship with a startup, but he also knew the two founders were recent MBA alumni from his university who had just landed a deal with Mark Cuban.

2. Find out what work interns do. Established companies likely have a clear list of job duties for their interns. Startups, almost by definition, need more Jack-of-all-trades interns. It's important when you interview and evaluate internship opportunities that you know what the job duties entail. While it's ok and expected for there to be some ambiguity and flexibility, you need to ensure the experience will be meaningful and you won't only be fetching coffee and making copies. It's fair to ask "What will I walk away from this internship having gained?" or "While I know in a startup there is no such thing as a typical day, can you tell me what last week would have looked like for a person in this position so I can get a feel for the expectations and experience?"

3. Make sure you get paid. The idea of completing a fully unpaid internship is very suspect. Very few unpaid opportunities are truly putting your best interests first. Yes you'd "just" be an "intern," but as an intern you should still be creating real value and thus be compensated in some manner. Remember:

Established companies with major name recognition pay their interns. Unfortunately, however, there are many small businesses trying to get free labor via interns. For a startup intern it's not unheard of to take on an unpaid assignment, but be guarded. Unpaid work should be short in duration and benefit you in some meaningful way (e.g., create an opportunity to expand your portfolio, enable you to meet and network with your target market or high profile potential employers, or pay for your expenses to attend a meaningful trade conference).

4. Write an outcome statement. Before you begin your internship search process, take time to write down the outcomes you hope to achieve from an internship. Then, as you interview for internships, take the information you gather from the interview and compare it to your initial goals. Force yourself to answer the following prompt in one sentence: "Upon completion of this internship I will have…" Share the sentence with your supervisor, print it and keep it at your desk, and ensure as time progresses that you are on track (or off track but in an good way).

5. Be sure you answer these questions:

- The Industry:
    - Is this opportunity in an industry that excites me?
    - Is it an industry in which I could see myself launching a company?
- The Model:
    - Can I sketch the core business model of the startup?
    - Is it a model that is scalable?
    - Is it a model I'm excited by?
    - Is the model easily replicable?
- The People:
    - Will I be working with really smart people?
    - Are these people who can help connect me to key players in the industry?
    - Are these people themselves key players in the industry?
- The Job:
    - Are the job duties going to push me out of my comfort zone?
    - Will I gain new and meaningful experience?
    - Is at least 60% of my time going to be spent on

developing new skills?
- Will I have a meaningful impact on the startup's performance?
- The Career Impact:
  - What are their former interns doing today?
  - What gap in my experience will this internship fill?
  - Will this experience help me launch my own startup, and how so?

Internships at startups can be great experiences, especially if you take the time to find the right opportunity and make the most of it. Like Claire noted, many startups are still very much in the formative stage, so regardless of whether or not you ultimately want to be involved in a startup on a full-time basis, they can be great opportunities to learn how and why businesses work the way they do. This means there is often much potential for personal and professional growth if you find the right opportunity.

If you consider all of the above and are still on the fence about whether to accept a particular internship, use Brian's money-where-your-mouth-is test to make the final decision: If you'd be willing to put your money on the line as an investment, then it's an opportunity worth pursuing.

Up until mid-2015 there was an awesome website called Remote Internships which curated a list of short-term, often paid internships with startups that students could complete from anywhere. It was brilliant in that you, the student in Peoria or Birmingham or Tulsa, could take on a short-term intern project with a Silicon Valley high-growth or venture-backed startup and get paid for the work you did in the process. A remote internship, by my definition, is a paid short-term and project-based opportunity in which you act like an independent contractor, but do so with an intern title from a location of your choosing.

In April of 2015 the Remote Internships team sent out an email notifying subscribers they were merging Remote Internships with their flagship company Founders Grid, a weekly newsletter for startup founders. On foundersgrid.com you can look at the job board, but in my opinion it now appears to focus more on tech jobs than internships. That said, if a remote internship is appealing to you, opportunities still occasionally arise on the board. Moreover, nothing is stopping you from pitching a remote intern concept to startups. (That's the entrepreneurial thing to do, after all.)

"The Three Asses Rule: a smart-ass team with a kick-ass product in a big-ass market."

– Jeff Clavier
Founder, SoftTech Venture Capital

Picking a Startup Team

Eric Liguori

Identifying real problems, staying flexible, and getting creative enough to generate viable solutions only happens when the right people are in place to make it happen. The testaments of countless successful entrepreneurs confirm that the team is one of the most important, if not the most important, aspect of the startup. The challenge in a classroom environment is teams are typically assigned or arbitrarily chosen. We'll table the "assigned" scenario for now as it is unfortunately beyond your control and focus on situations where you get to pick your team.

All too often teams are selected by picking the four closest humans to you at the time. To combat this tendency, I created a pitch contest team formation process modeled off of Startup Weekend's idea selection process. Every student pitches an idea, and every student then votes on the top three ideas they want to work on. Those who pitched the top six or seven ideas then chat with other students to form teams for the project (assuming a 30-person class with four-person teams, on average).

The past year has proven my process to be ineffective and flawed. First, students who pitch well may pitch a terrible idea, or even worse the diamonds in the rough may get overlooked because their pitches were not compelling. Next, one honors student told me a few weeks back his strategy was to do an "ok pitch" so he would not win. His logic was simple: If he had a winning pitch, people would jump on his team, leaving him with no choice in the matter. If his pitch was not selected, however, he could pick the idea to work on based on the team. He argued, and rightfully so, that he had a lot more risk in his grade if he spent the semester working on a major project with a bad group than just losing a few points for having an average and somewhat less than compelling pitch. He was right, and in trying to prevent one bad team-picking situation I inadvertently created another one.

Unfortunately, there's no silver bullet here. I have one colleague who gives the entire class a personality test and then creates groups by ranking students from high to low on conscientiousness and then grouping them in order. (The most conscientious students get grouped together, and the least conscientious students get grouped together.) I have another colleague who believes students are not competent enough to choose ideas themselves, so she brings in "experts" from the business community to listen to the pitches and select the best ideas for the student groups to pursue. (This method possibly could help mitigate the risk of overlooking the diamond in the rough, but its foundational logic is flawed: You're too incompetent to pick the idea, but you're competent enough to work on the idea some random "expert" picks for you, even if it's not one you are interested in or passionate about?)

The lack of a miracle solution to classroom team formation stems from the fact that everyone enrolled in a class must be part of a team. Why teams you ask? The answer is simple: Almost all entrepreneurial ventures require a team; the myth of the lone solo-preneur is, at best, an outlier. Jeff Clavier, founder of SoftTech Venture Capital, has a "Three Asses" rule for entrepreneurial success: "[You need] a smart-ass team building a kick-ass product in a big-ass market." Clavier goes on to note that "when you factor all the ingredients (and a bit of luck) that are necessary to lead a startup from inception to a successful outcome, however big or small, the founders make up more than half of these." Personally, I'm fortunate to teach at The University of Tampa where we have an incredibly smart student population, so in theory my classes should, by default, always consist of 100% "smart-ass teams." Yet somehow this doesn't happen. Somewhere along the line the math breaks and the cumulative sum of smart-ass people is not necessarily a smart-ass team.

$$\text{Smart-ass person + Smart-ass person + Smart-ass person}$$
$$\neq$$
$$\text{Smart-ass team (necessarily)}$$

Building a smart-ass team is difficult at best in optimal situations and nearly impossible when faced with virtually no resources and a limited candidate pool (your classmates) from which to choose. Your challenge as an entrepreneurial leader is to work your "smart ass" off to find classmates who will join your team because your passion for the idea is contagious and your leadership style is motivating. But that's no small task, and certainly it is easier said than done. Having seen the team formation process unfold countless times in countless ways, here are four factors you should consider as you build a within-class startup team:

1. Grades matter
The grade you will receive on your project matters to most, but not all,

students. It goes without saying that picking team members who share similar grade ideals as yourself will save you a lot of frustration later on, but it's not always that simple. One semester I asked each of the pitch winners why their peers should choose to join their team over all the others. The first student said "because I plan to get an 'A'" and so the next six students answered the question the exact same way. Everyone will tell you they both want and plan to work hard enough to earn an "A" when it's team formation time, so be bold: Ask people what their GPAs are; ask them how they would approach solving the most pressing problem your idea is facing; and look for people you've had other classes with that are known commodities.

2. Grades don't matter

Ok, now the flip side of that argument. Grades matter, but the grade your project gets is not always in line with the progress you made on your business. In fact, I'd guess most students spend a lot of time jumping through unavoidable grade hoops at the expense of making meaningful progress on core aspects of their business. Dr. Bob Justis gave Todd Graves a failing grade on his business plan and said it would never work. Justis is a leading expert on global franchising; his textbooks on the subject are used around the globe. Today Graves' company, Raising Canes, is a wild success grossing over $100,000,000 annually with 225+ locations. In picking a team you need to make sure your priorities align with those of your teammates. Be honest and let them know progress is more important to you than your final grade. In doing so, you'll attract likeminded talent and make great strides, but it may be at the expense of getting a top-notch grade.

3. Diversity matters

In his 2016 address at the World Economic Forum, Canadian Prime Minister Trudeau stated, "Diversity is the engine of invention; it generates creativity that enriches the world." Data from leading global consultancy McKinsey & Company both confirms and quantifies Trudeau's assertion. McKinsey found that diversity pays a dividend: Gender-diversity results in a 15% likelihood you will financially outperform your less diverse competitors, and ethnic diversity raises that number to 35%. In this context, however, I'm talking not just about gender and ethnic diversity, but also about skill diversity. When you can, get students from different majors involved. A marketing major, a mechanical engineering major, an entrepreneurship major, and a finance major is a great combination. That's four people with different skill sets, each of which likely approach problem solving differently and cover a wide variety of content areas. Remember, diversity pays dividends.

4. Divide and conquer is a terrible idea

You cannot build a successful team by planning from the onset to execute on each portion of the business model separately in silos. Successful startups take a synchronized and collaborative effort. Ask potential teammates how they solve problems. Ask them how they prefer to work and how they prefer to communicate. Explain to them why collaboration is key. You need to get a feel for whether or not this person will be a collaborative and compatible team member. I'd normally censor myself, but we're past that point in this entry, so here goes nothing: At the end of the day, nobody wants to work with an asshole no matter how good they are.

"Always do your best. What you plant now, you will harvest later."

– Og Mandino
Author, *The Greatest Salesman in the World*

It's OK to Get a Job...

Eric Liguori

Graduation sneaks up on everyone. I finished my undergraduate degree unusually quickly, and upon looking back I regret not sticking around for at least another football season, if not longer. Regardless of your personal timeline, graduation forces everyone to finally come to terms with reality and answer the difficult questions you've been putting off for the duration of your career as an entrepreneurship student: Do you move forward and launch the venture you've been working on as a class project, or do you pivot? Do you look at different new venture opportunities? Conventional wisdom says the correct answer to at least one of these questions is "yes," thus implying that responding with an answer of "no, I'm going to get a job working for someone else" is incorrect.

Perhaps conventional logic is sound. As a recent graduate you've not yet come to expect the income and lifestyle of a full-time working professional; at this stage in your life, you're probably still totally OK with a low-cost college apartment full of roommates and Friday nights full of bad pizza and cheap domestic beer. (Maybe that's an extreme characterization, but you get the point.) There's merit to taking on the risk of failure when you have little to lose, especially if you have an idea you are passionate about and think can scale – go for it, and more power to you!

If the above applies to you, stop reading this entry now and skip ahead. (Your cheap domestic beer is probably getting warm anyway.) The rest of this article is here to tell you it's OK to take a job working for the man and opt for a stable income while you get some experience and figure things out. Yes, it's completely OK...as long as you have a plan in place that gets you where you want to be in 5-7 years.

Students are, in some ways, predestined to fail in entrepreneurial ventures. Sure there are countless success stories of successful student startups, and sure there are no guarantees either way, but think about it from an ecological perspective: The organism with the fewest resources and the least experience in a given environment is the most likely to be eliminated first. And the organism that has matured for a few years, built up a cache of resources, and gained some experience (and a better taste in pizza and beer) is likely to be the one doing the eliminating. Taking the right job with a predetermined plan in place could very much set you on the path to being the latter organism, the one that survives and even thrives.

Here are a few words of wisdom for those of you on the "working for someone else" route:

First, remember you're only doing this to develop a toolbox of adaptable and universally valuable business skills you'll be able to use to launch your own venture in the future. Furthermore, make sure the job you select allows you to fully develop these skills in a timely manner. Let's take management skills as an example. Management skills like hiring/firing practices, familiarity with federal labor laws, and payroll management are a great thing to learn during your time off of the entrepreneurial grid. They're useful in nearly every new venture you may undertake, and there's likely not an investor out there who is willing to put capital behind someone with no management experience.

Second, when taking the job route, you should be sure the job opportunity you pursue helps you develop experience and grow your network in the industry in which you wish to start your new venture. John Morrow, serial entrepreneur and entrepreneur in residence at USF St. Petersburg, recently told me that one of the biggest hurdles student entrepreneurs must overcome is a lack of industry knowledge, as students can really only gain such knowledge by actively working in the industry. A lack of industry experience means a lack of the social capital needed to help your startup succeed; it means you'll be blindly making guesses at what industry trends may be (or, at best, that you'll be making educated guesses based on secondhand experience or information) and that your idea from day one will likely be under-developed and under-informed in comparison to those of industry insiders. If you are one of the lucky ones able to land a job in the industry of your choosing, be sure to take full advantage of the networking opportunities inherent in industry and trade association events and mixers. Get whatever industry standard certifications are available. Build out your LinkedIn profile and connect with everyone you meet. Begin establishing credibility for yourself in the industry, and be sure you are always a consummate professional as your reputation is on the line!

Third, use the time you spend as someone else's full-time employee to pay off your debts (credit cards, car payments, student loans, etc.) and save up some cash. Here's an important data point for you to remember: The number one source of funding for most young companies is the founder's personal savings. A 2015 Gallup poll found that 68% of Americans believed that not having enough personal savings played a key role in their decision to not start a business, so if you want to launch a startup in the future it's imperative you plan and save now. Moving forward, the second most common source of funding for young startups is credit cards. This has two implications for you: (1) You may eventually need your available credit to survive, so pay it down now while you have the chance, and (2) given that every $1,000 in credit card debt used by a new firm increases the chances they will fail by 2.2%, having cash in the bank to reduce your dependency on credit strengthens your odds of success.

This brings us to the topic of credit scores. If you don't have credit established by now, or if you are unfortunate enough to have bad credit, you're already behind the curve. Your credit score is a sign of your conscientiousness and is your financial track record. Low credit scores turn off potential investors and banks, and credit card companies won't raise credit limits or lower interest rates for those with poor or no credit. A credit score is easy to tarnish, but thankfully it's also easy(ish) to fix, albeit not quick. If you've already made some mistakes, now's the time to go on the offensive, get some credit counseling, and turn that ship around.

Fourth and finally, you need to have a plan for accomplishing all of the above, and once you do, you've got to pursue it with intense focus and determination. Remember that intensity begets greatness. Everything is not going to simply fall in place; you're going to have to work to make it happen using a combination of focus and discipline. If you fail to execute your plan, you're wasting a valuable opportunity to set yourself up for future venture success. But if you succeed, you've got worlds of opportunity waiting for you.

Some great resources on where new ventures get funding:
- http://www.kauffman.org/what-we-do/research/kauffman-firm-survey-series/the-use-of-credit-card-debt-by-new-firms
- http://www.kauffman.org/multimedia/sketchbook/kauffman-sketchbook-money-game

---

Repeat after me:
"I am exceptional. I am exceptional. I am exceptional."

Exactly, you are exceptional. You are so exceptional you do not represent the world at large. You need to go out and see what the world thinks of your idea.

Learning From Your Peers
Eric Liguori

In 2015 I set a goal to talk to a number of rockstar students engaged in entrepreneurship programs around the nation. I sent emails to my colleagues at many of the top programs across the country and asked them to give me a list of their most successful students, whom I then set out to interview. I wanted to find out what these top performers did differently and what advice they had for their fellow students. What follows is a curated panel discussion of insights from five awesome aspiring entrepreneurs/intrapreneurs. Enjoy!

The Student Panelists

Tanner Agar is the CEO and founder of The Chef Shelf, a venture he launched while a student at Texas Christian University (TCU). Agar is also the founder of Brüd Food, a company he started in October 2014 that works with breweries to create salsas, mustards, and barbeque sauces inspired by their signature beers. As a student, Agar was active in TCU's CEO club and competed in both the TCU and CEO National Elevator Pitch Competitions. Connect with Tanner at tanner.agar@thechefshelf.com and check out www.thechefshelf.com the next time you need to send a great gift or order some good eats.

Jenny Amaraneni is the co-founder/CEO of SOLO Eyewear, a line of eco-friendly sunglasses that donates proceeds from each pair sold to fund eye care for people in need. (To date, SOLO has helped over 14,000 people across 30+ countries.) The *San Diego Business Journal* named Amaraneni one of its Top 25 in Their 20's in 2013, and *San Diego Magazine* included her on its 2013 Top 50 People to Watch list. She has an undergraduate degree from Louisiana State University (2007) and a MBA from San Diego State University (2011). Be sure to order your next pair of sunglasses from SOLO at www.soloeyewear.com.

Renan de Lima graduated in May 2015 from California State University, Fresno. As a student, de Lima was a longstanding officer in Fresno State's Collegiate Entrepreneurs' Organization, during which time he helped lead the chapter to formal recognition at both the campus and national levels. He remains an active Startup Weekend Community Organizer still today. Currently de Lima works as an Associate Financial Analyst at the corporate headquarters of E & J Gallo Winery, the world's largest producer and distributor of wine and spirits.

Raul Hernandez Ochoa is a student at San Diego State University. Ochoa is a Lavin Entrepreneur Fellow who has worked in SDSU's Life Sciences Entrepreneurship Program and has also participated in several live small business and industry consulting projects through SDSU's Lavin Center. He received the prestigious Larry and Madeline Petersen Endowed Scholarship in Entrepreneurship in 2013.

Erick Rodriguez is the president of the Entrepreneurship Club at the University of Florida. He is also a Google Intern, owns his own small e-retailing business, and is a graduate of Harvard's Summer Venture in Management Program. Under his leadership the UF Entrepreneurship Club has had members both compete in and win a variety of competitions around the nation, including the 2015 Southeastern Entrepreneurship Conference in which UF students took two of the top three spots.

The Panel Discussion

Question 1: What on-campus resources have you taken advantage of?

Tanner: I took advantage of everything that I possibly could. The first one, and this is one that everyone should be able to use, is just the faculty. I found, in general, that a lot of people who become college professors really care about the students and want to help them, and a lot of times they don't really get asked. People don't engage with their professors because they don't want to bother them or because they think, "Wow, he is so accomplished he wouldn't want to talk to me." But I found, actually, the professors really do want to talk to you. They want to help you. I can literally walk into their office and say, "Here are my problems, and I would like to stay until we fix them," and they are like "Oh, OK, that's cool." These people ran companies like Ancestry and AOL; they are incredible. Besides just the professors, TCU has some great programs. We've got an entrepreneurship club, which is fantastic. We've got access to a technology incubator, and it's actually through the TCU incubator that all my office space is paid for, which is awesome… I've gone to 3 business plan competitions now, and TCU sponsored me for all of those. I've really gotten so much help from the university.

Raul: The Lavin program, the Lavin Center. I am constantly in there talking to professors, asking to be connected with alumni, community leaders. I think it is really awesome to be able to do that as a student. I get to go to a lot of community entrepreneurship events for free. I get to expand my network and learn what other people are doing here in San Diego.

Renan: Most of the resources that I have taken advantage of are in the Lyles Center, the entrepreneurship center at Fresno State. I've been a part of the Collegiate Entrepreneurs' Organization for the last couple years serving as the Special Activities Director, and we hold a lot of special events for students on campus. Right now we are focused on hosting another entrepreneurship networking night. We've also hosted startup weekend on campus, and because of this I was able to attend UP Summit in Las Vegas, an international event meant to generate economic development through entrepreneurship.

Jenny: So there were a number of things that I did. The entrepreneurship center on our campus offered a series of workshops for students who were interested in launching companies, including workshops on ideation, presentations, and business plans. So I attended those workshops, and I leveraged the connection of the entrepreneurship center in the community and started going to networking events. A lot of the entrepreneurial organizations in San Diego would give tickets to the entrepreneurship center for students to attend, and that helped in networking and connecting me with more experienced people. I also turned to professors and advisors for advice. All of those were really critical in giving me the confidence to (1) start a company, and (2) actively pursue launching it.

Question 2: What helped you most from your academic training?

Renan: I think, as a finance major, I really chose the major because I wanted to get a better understanding of the fundamental principles of value creation. I really wanted to understand business, and I think the finance major here at Fresno State does a pretty good job of equipping you with the skills you need to transition into the workforce. I had an internship last summer with Rabobank where I worked as a financial analyst for them, and in a lot of the things I did as a financial analyst, whether it was spreading financial statements or underwriting loans and working with a loan officer,

61

I was using a lot of the skills that I learned from the textbook or on Excel, things like that, to get the work done.

Tanner: I came to TCU because I wanted to major in entrepreneurship. And I think that that just inherently made a great… I mean, I had professors who understood [entrepreneurship], who came from that world and who know how to manage that, and they taught in a way that kind of appealed to that mindset. A lot of my core classes were "OK, here's the lecture, and here's the textbook, and you're going to listen, and you're going to take an exam." But TCU really did a great job. That's just not how an entrepreneurship classes were run. They're discussion-based, problem-based. I would say it's very easy for me to buy a textbook and to read it to myself. I don't need a professor for that. I don't need a classroom. It's the value of the ideas not only coming from the professor in a discussion, but also the students. The students are really one of the best resources you have because most of them will be smart, they get excited about a project, and they've got time to talk about it and to develop it.

Erick: So I have a good quote here. Let's see… so according to the Carnegie Institute of Technology, 85% of your financial success is due to your personality and ability to communicate, negotiate, and lead. Shockingly only 15% is due to technical knowledge. And so when I entered the University of Florida, I had never been much of an academic or a very studious person, so I knew that was not an area where I had a competitive advantage and was going to really differentiate myself. This is why I got very involved with extracurriculars and entrepreneur activities. I knew that was going to be what was going to differentiate myself.

Question 3: What have you done to differentiate yourself from your peers to maximize opportunities?

Tanner: Right. What's made me successful in my business is that I have just focused on it. I focused on it like other people just won't. I never joined a fraternity. I don't have cable. I don't really follow sports. There are just so many things that people spend their time with. I don't really party very much. From a college male standpoint, I'm pretty boring. I remember thinking this in college, like everybody comes in on Monday, and they're like "Oh dude, this awesome party! After we went to the Cowboys game!" and I was like "Oh yeah! OK." "What did you do?" "I stayed up really late working on this cool thing." And they're like, "Oh, nice. Great story." I like working. I wanted to work, and so that focus has made me successful, but it always comes at a cost. You know, most people look back on college and they're like, "Oh, all this cool stuff I do with my frat brothers." I don't have any of those stories, but I don't regret it at the same time. It's just different.

Renan: I took advantage of internships. Nowadays as a business major you need to do that in order to differentiate yourself when you are going out into the labor force. I worked for a financial advisory firm during the summer of my sophomore/junior year and then I worked for Rabobank bank my junior/senior year. I also worked as junior research analyst for Regency Investment Advisors and was involved with a couple of organizations here on campus, including the Collegiate Entrepreneurs' Organization and the Financial Management Association. Through these organizations I've been able to go to a lot of different conferences, compete in pitch competitions, help host a lot of cool events, and facilitate a lot of cool things.

Raul: I'm surrounded by great peers to be honest with you. The one thing that I think I do differently has been taking advantage of opportunities, continuing reaching out to people, and also just being hungry. I just want to make something work and see what I can do and create.

Erick: Whenever I enter a class I usually try to sit in the front or second row. I try to be very interactive. So from the first day, I try to get to know the faculty member, the professor, because aside from the academic knowledge that the professor might be able to share, the professor also has, most likely, a lot of resources, connections, networks that he can help you with. One of my entrepreneurship professors connected me with a current Google employee who will potentially be a mentor for my future career progression. And so, trying to make the most of the entrepreneurial classes, trying to really pick the brain of the faculty member aside from just what they share from the books and through lecturing, that's how I maximize the classes.

Question 4: What would you tell a new freshman wanting to get the most their entrepreneurship program to look for, do, or seek out?

Tanner: I would say that tons and tons of people want to be the person with an idea. It's very cool to be the guy; it's cool to be Mark Zuckerberg. However, if you sit in your home trying to think of your idea so then you will feel validated to go join this entrepreneurial community, you are never going to be able to join it. Most people involved in startups did not think of the idea, but they are paramount to being involved with it. So I would say the first thing you should do is get connected into the environment however you can. The environment is pretty generous, I mean pretty open as far as I've seen. You want to come and hang out at the happy hours and you want to talk to people about what they are doing? Perfect. You want to say, "Hey, I kind of know a little bit about something like that. Maybe I could just kind of program that for you." Perfect. You can get yourself involved at kind of a very low, minimum level and explore it and find out what it's about. And when you are around these people is when you will either find an idea of someone else's you can latch onto, or you will kind of discover your idea. But you can't sit around at home staring at your computer hoping your eureka moment finds you. You have to go out and engage with these people. And at least in the groups I'm in, I've never seen them turn somebody away who was earnestly trying to find out about this kind of community and this lifestyle and this career path.

Raul: First, to figure out themselves. To see where they stand, and not to focus on a major but focus on a mission. Tim Brown, the CEO of IDEO, mentions something really interesting in an article: Students, when they go to school, when they choose what school, they shouldn't think about a major. They should think, "What's my mission, what do I do, what do I want to solve?" because when you can answer these questions the domain of major and school fall into place. Students need to figure out themselves, their goals and priorities, and what they have to do to get there. And then take all the opportunities that you can. Don't take regular courses. Take courses that are experience- or activity-based. Work in the community. Get involved with clubs and organizations. Not just any organization, but really get involved. Create a core peer group of students that you like to work with.

Erick: If I was speaking to someone who was entering the University of Florida, or any academic institution for the first time, the things I would share would be the lessons learned through my experiences. First, maintain a good GPA, at least a 3.5, but you are not going to set yourself apart from others just by GPA. I would recommend getting involved, perhaps by joining 2 or 3 organizations throughout your university career. Get to know your peers. You don't know what you don't know. You don't know what or who your peers may know, and they can help you. Always think in terms of how you can help the other person, and then naturally help and value will return to you. Make the most of classes. Perform well, but most of all get to know your professors. You never know when you will need a letter of recommendation, or just a mentor or advisor or friend. And as far as entrepreneurship goes, that's a tricky thing. It's a wandering path. Sometimes it can be lonely. Sometimes you're like the lone wolf in entrepreneurship. But getting involved in an entrepreneurship club on campus is a fantastic opportunity to find that 1% of people who are actually interested in this. Once you're engaged, look for the doers. There's people who say and there's people who do. There's people who share ideas all the time; ideas are plentiful. Then there's people who do, and they're like, "You know, I had this idea, and I did this, I implemented this, I have results, I have figures." Those are the people you want to associate yourself with, befriend, and learn from. And hopefully become one. A doer, and not a sayer.

Jenny: I always tell students to milk it. When you're a student, that's your ticket. You're able to open so many doors and meet with so many individuals in the community both on and off campus. So really take advantage of being a student. Identify who it is that you admire, who is it, that leading company that you want to connect with and reach out to them, and let them know, "Hey, I'm a student at blah blah blah, and I really admire what you're doing, can I sit down with you for 30 minutes, buy you a cup of coffee and learn more about your journey?" And nine times out of ten you will get that meeting and establish a connection that can help you for the rest of your life.

Renan: That's a good, yeah that's a really good question. So as a freshman coming in I would say get in touch with all of your professors, and especially all of the entrepreneurship professors. Find out what they are interested in, see if it matches what you are interested in, and build a relationship with them. Your end goal is to start a business, right? It's to have a startup, and you should be able to achieve that at the end of your four-year education. You want to meet as many professors as possible, find a professor who you can build a relationship with, discover some of the classes you can take that will allow you to build that business that you want, and then do it. It gets to a point where you have to make progress. You have to do something, and college is the perfect time for you to do that. I went a different path. And looking back on it now, I probably would have made some changes to it. I would have loved to have founded a startup while in college, but when it comes down to it, I didn't for several reasons. I talked about, kind of, how I was so focused on school that I didn't allow myself to work on any other projects. I really do think that was kind of a hindrance. If I look back on it now and I list the regrets of going through my four-year education, not having a startup is definitely at the top of the list.

Part 2

Bolstering Your Entrepreneurial Mindset

"What's amazing about what we're doing is that there aren't any rules. We're making them up as we go."

– Christina Stembel
Founder, Farmgirl Flowers

I Am a CEO
Kathryn Sowa

"The only thing that separates you from the successful entrepreneurs of the world is time and effort. Anything that they can do, you can do. Too many people see great entrepreneurs or greatness in general as some kind of special thing that has to be assigned them. Nothing could be further from the truth. Every entrepreneur feels like an impostor at one time or another. All entrepreneurs are trying to be better versions of themselves."

–Dr. Isaiah Hankel

Like many entrepreneurs, I've worked on a number of failed ideas during my career, some my own and some not. Hindsight is 20/20, and now that I'm a little older and wiser, I realize that a lack of self-confidence was the biggest contributor to many of my own ideas never getting off of the ground. At the time, I wrongly assumed I needed more experience or someone else's approval to move forward, when in fact I only needed the confidence to know I was the right one to get the job done.

Over the years, I've worked with hundreds of students facing confidence crises similar to mine. It's tough to deal with that second-guessing voice inside our head, and everyone doubts themselves at one point or another. Great leaders and entrepreneurs may ooze confidence now, but even their success stories took time to develop. No matter your situation, the only thing stopping you from building your dream company, being the CEO, and turning your passion into a reality is a lack of confidence in your ability to make it happen.

You've probably heard the saying "trust your gut" many times before, and there's a good reason why: It's great advice. Confidence really is key. You need to believe in yourself and your abilities to be the best person for your company. As Theodore Roosevelt famously said, "Believe you can, and you're halfway there." You don't have to have all the answers right now, but you do have to believe that you can figure it out along the way. Developing the trust and confidence you have in yourself is just as important as developing your skills or growing your startup. After all, if you don't believe in yourself, who will?

Do you remember when you learned to ride a bike? First came the training wheels, which provided some guidance and stability to get you started. But then there came a point when you had to take them off. How on earth were you supposed to balance on only two wheels? What if the road wasn't smooth? What if you fell?

But you went for it anyway.

At first it was tricky, learning to steer and balance. You probably fell or crashed a few times, but you dusted yourself off and got back on that bike. The more you practiced, the easier it got, and eventually you were able to fly down the street and feel a new sense of freedom to go places you never imagined.

Riding a bike is a lot like entrepreneurship.

Being in school is your training wheels - you're gaining valuable knowledge and have an incredible support system at your disposal. You're learning the fundamentals and the tools you'll need for the future. But when the training wheels come off, you enter the real world, and it's scary. What if you don't know what to do? What if you make the wrong decision? What if you fail? Guess what, all three of these things will probably happen. But with persistence and determination, soon you will start to figure things out along the way, just like all the entrepreneurs before you have done. As with your bike, entrepreneurship will give you the freedom to pursue your passions and go places you never imagined possible.

But only if you believe that you can do it.

5 Tips for Building Confidence

Even though you know it's possible, how can you actually build your confidence? Here are five tips that will help.

1. Be With the Best
You're the average of the five people you're around the most. Take a quick inventory of whom you've spent the most time with this past week. Who are they? Are they positive, motivating forces? Do you respect and admire them? If not, find a new top five.

Surround yourself with good people who can push you to be better and do bigger things. This has helped me focus on moving forward and has even motivated me to decide to leave behind unfavorable situations. Whether mentors, co-founders, teammates, fellow entrepreneurs, or friends, make sure to spend your time with people who understand where you're coming from and can help you get to where you want to go.

2. Set Strong Goals

Studies show that writing down and visualizing your goals is a powerful tool. According to business coach Tony Brooks, committing your goals to paper and regularly reviewing them gives you a 95% higher chance of achieving your desired outcomes. Entrepreneur Ryan Allis feels likewise, as he commonly advises fellow entrepreneurs to write down their short- and long-term goals, frame them, and put them in a visible place where they can serve as a daily reminder.

3. Put Yourself Out There

One important way to build confidence is through experience. There are so many opportunities out there to get your feet wet in the entrepreneurial community and develop your CEO skill set. Getting involved in community events will force you to get out of your comfort zone and meet other people who have had similar experiences to yours. Once you start creating a broader network of entrepreneurs and entrepreneurial experiences, you'll realize that if others are doing it, you can too!

Some national entrepreneurship opportunities to explore:

> **National CEO Conference (www.c-e-o.org)**
> Each year, the Collegiate Entrepreneurs' Organization (CEO) hosts the largest national conference for student entrepreneurs. Over 1,000 students from schools around the world come together to network, learn, and be inspired by top entrepreneurs. From keynote speakers to workshops and networking opportunities, attendees gain valuable insight into advancing their own ideas and companies.
>
> The CEO conference also features the National Elevator Pitch Competition in which the top 60 students have 90 seconds to pitch their business or idea to panels of investors and judges. Winners receive national exposure and cash prizes, and previous first-place finishers have even appeared on ABC's *Shark Tank*.

GSEA (www.eonetwork.org/eo-gsea)

The Global Student Entrepreneur Awards (GSEA), which is part of the Entrepreneurs' Organization (EO), is a global competition for undergraduate and graduate students who are also business owners. Students compete against their peers from around the world in regional competitions to earn the right to advance to the national and then the global competition. Students not only receive great exposure and connections, but they can also win business services, mentorship opportunities, and cash prizes.

Startup Weekend (startupweekend.org)

Want to get the feel of the entrepreneurial experience by building a business in 54 hours? Then check out a Startup Weekend. Whether you already have your own idea or simply want to join a team for the weekend, Startup Weekend gives you hands-on experience in working to build and pitch a viable product. Whether you win or not, it's a great way to gain some real entrepreneurial experience in a short period of time.

Accelerators and Fellowships

Startup accelerators are programs designed to foster rapid growth among the companies in their portfolios. Startups apply to accelerator programs with the hope of being accepted and gaining access to seed funding, mentorship, and other valuable resources, all typically in exchange for a percentage of equity in the company. The accelerator process is a brief one, typically only lasting about three months before the startup once again goes out on its own. A few popular accelerator programs include Y Combinator (www.ycombinator.com), Techstars (www.techstars.com), Impact Engine (theimpactengine.com), and the EO Accelerator (www.eonetwork.org/eo-accelerator).

Like accelerators, fellowships are programs also geared toward helping entrepreneurs take their companies and careers to the next level through education, mentorship, collaboration, and networking with other talented and motivated fellows. Each fellowship has its own set of requirements, application processes, and program structures. Some popular fellowships include the Thiel Fellowship (www.thielfellowship.org), the Founder Institute (http://fi.co/), and the Founders Fellowship (www.collegefounders.org).

Co-Working Spaces

A co-working space is a local shared working environment in which individuals from various industries and/or companies work within a single communal space. Co-working spaces give entrepreneurs the opportunity to network with like-minded individuals and gain access to resources that they might not have been able to access on their own.

4. Superhero Stance

Did you know your body language has a profound impact on how others view you as well as how you feel? In "Your Body Language Shapes Who You Are," a TED talk that I consider to be one of the best ever, social psychologist Amy Cuddy professes the power of body language. (You can search for this talk and many more on TED.com; the direct URL to Cuddy's talk is provided in the references.) As part of her presentation, Amy shared how "power posing" – standing in a posture of confidence – can affect chemical levels in your brain that impact your chances for success. The next time you're feeling nervous, stand like Superman for two minutes, with your feet apart, back straight, hands on hips, and head up. I guarantee this power pose will help trick your mind out of its doubting and instill a new sense of confidence in you.

5. Celebrate Successes

Knowing you're working toward achieving your goals is also important for building confidence. Celebrate your successes! Be proud of yourself when you finish your to-do list or when you secure that new customer. Take time to appreciate the progress you make on a daily basis. Follow John Brubaker's philosophy of having a 3x5 rule: Every day, journal three successes you have achieved by five p.m., no matter how small they may be. Then, occasionally reread your entries for a boost of confidence and inspiration. You'll never get to the big crowning achievements without going through the smaller steps.

As Henry Ford said, "Whether you think you can or whether you think you can't, you're right." In the end, your success comes down to you and whether you have the confidence in yourself to achieve your dreams. Being confident may be the hardest part of your journey, but at the end of the day, the only person you can truly rely on is you, so invest in yourself and believe in the power you have to do whatever you want.

There are few people who have worked harder at the national level to advance student entrepreneurship than Katie Sowa. Over the better part of the last decade, she's worked to support tens of thousands of college entrepreneurs around the globe.

We often discuss the importance of having an entrepreneurial mindset, noting traits such as opportunity recognition, risk taking, and creativity. Yet too often we underestimate the value of confidence. In his book, *Become a Key Person of Influence*, Daniel Priestly writes about resourcefulness, noting "resourcefulness shows up AFTER you make a commitment." Making a commitment to execute without resources is difficult, which is why you need to be confident in yourself, your idea, and your ability to execute. As Priestly says, "The [successful] people I know over-commit themselves then figure it all out later." Are you confident enough to take on the world of the startup entrepreneur?

"None of us is smarter than all of us, and much of the time you accomplish great things by listening to other people."

– Patrick Snyder
Executive Director, United States Association for Small Business & Entrepreneurship

You Are Not Special

Eric Liguori

I love a good commencement speech, and there's no shortage of them on YouTube. A few years ago I was lucky enough to stumble upon David McCullough, Jr.'s address to the Wellesley High Class of 2012 which he fondly titled "You Are Not Special." The content was witty, spot-on, and relevant to any aspiring entrepreneur, so I adapted it into a startup-framed LinkedIn post, which incidentally has become my most viewed and successful posting to date.

Let's stop and do some math for a moment. The National Center for Education Statistics reports there are over 21,000 high schools and nearly 10,000 colleges in the U.S. alone. For ease's sake, let's assume each high school holds commencement annually, each college holds it bi-annually, and the average commencement speaker talks for 19 minutes. That equates to 12,983 hours (541 days) of commencement addresses each year. Luckily for you, I've saved you from the mind-numbing task of trying to sort through and listen to it all by putting together a recap of my favorite entrepreneurship-relevant quotes from the best speakers and speeches.

David McCullough, Jr.

1. "You are one in a million on a planet of 6.8 billion, meaning there are nearly 7,000 people just like you." Ideas are worthless; it's absolutely about execution.

2. "Learn enough to recognize how little you know." As Eric Ries points out, "A startup's job is to rigorously measure where it is right now, confronting the hard truths that assessment reveals, and then devise experiments to learn how to move the real numbers closer to the ideal."

3. "Today is just the beginning; it is where you go from here that matters." Pivot as you need.

4. "Be worthy of your advantages, and work to cultivate them." Your time is better spent here than in fussing with bandaging your

weaknesses, a sentiment best outlined in Gallop's StrengthsFinder 2.0.

5. "Carpe the heck out of the diem. Get busy, have at it, don't wait for inspiration or passion to find you. Get up, get out, explore, find it yourself, grab hold with both hands." Entrepreneurship requires action, period.

6. Use real metrics. Don't blindly claim you're "one of the best so [you] can feel better about [y]ourselves and bask in a little easy distinction however vague and unverifiable. And count [y] ourselves among the elite, whoever they might be, and enjoy a perceived leg up on the perceived competition. The phrase 'one of the best' defies logic; by definition there can be only one best. You're it or you're not." Resist the easy comforts of complacency; challenge assumptions.

Jim Carrey

1. "It can be rough out there, but that's ok, because there's soft serve ice cream, with sprinkles." No matter how tough your day becomes, there's always a bright side.

2. "Now fear is going to be a player in your life, but you get to decide how much. You can spend your whole life imagining ghosts, worrying about the pathway to the future, but all there will ever be is what's happening here, and the decisions we make in this moment, which are based in either love or fear. So many of us choose our path out of fear disguised as practicality. What we really want seems impossibly out of reach and ridiculous to expect so we never dare to ask the universe for it. I'm saying I'm the proof that you can ask the universe for it."

3. "You can fail at what you don't want, so you might as well take a chance on doing what you love." In an earlier entry we discussed why it was OK to get a job even though you want to be an entrepreneur. The reality is sometimes finding a job is a necessary precursor to launching a startup, but if you have a founder's DNA, you may choose to take the bold step and launch your startup anyways. Failure happens on occasion to all of us;

you can resist failing at a startup by never trying, but then aren't you just failing at life?

4. "How will you serve the world? What do they need that your talent will provide? That's all you have to figure out." Once you truly identify how you create value for others, the rest of the business model should be much easier to sketch out. I'm not saying it will be easy to execute on, but at least you'll have a plan of attack from which you can work.

5. "I was concerned about going out into the world and doing something bigger than myself until someone smarter than myself made me realize that there is nothing bigger than myself. My soul is not contained within the limits of my body; my body is contained within the limitlessness of my soul." Don't be afraid of having a bold vision; instead, embrace the vision and work on execution.

Steve Jobs

1. "It was impossible to connect the dots looking forward when I was in college, but it was very, very clear looking backwards ten years later. Again, you can't connect the dots looking forward; you can only connect them looking backwards. So you have to trust that the dots will somehow connect in your future. You have to trust in something: your gut, destiny, life, karma, whatever. Because believing that the dots will connect down the road will give you the confidence to follow you heart even when it leads you off the well-worn path. And that will make all the difference."

2. "I didn't see it then, but it turned out that getting fired from Apple was the best thing that could have ever happened to me. The heaviness of being successful was replaced by the lightness of being a beginner again, less sure about everything…It was awful tasting medicine, but I guess the patient needed it. Sometimes life hits you in the head with a brick. Don't lose faith. I'm convinced that the only thing that kept me going was that I loved what I did. You've got to find what you love. And that is as true for your work as it is for your lovers. Your work is going to

fill a large part of your life, and the only way to be truly satisfied is to do what you believe is great work. And the only way to do great work is to love what you do. If you haven't found it yet, keep looking. Don't settle. As with all matters of the heart, you'll know when you find it."

3. "Remembering that you are going to die is the best way I know to avoid the trap of thinking you have something to lose. You are already naked. There is no reason not to follow your heart."

4. "Your time is limited, so don't waste it living someone else's life. Don't be trapped by dogma, which is living with the results of other people's thinking. Don't let the noise of others' opinions drown out your own inner voice. And most important, have the courage to follow your heart and intuition."

Admiral William H. McRaven

1. "Changing the world can happen anywhere, and anyone can do it."

2. "You can't change the world alone; you will need some help. And to truly get from your starting point to your destination takes friends, colleagues, the goodwill of strangers, and a strong coxswain to guide you. If you want to change the world, find someone to help you paddle." Startups are hard ships to steer alone; building the right team is critical to success, so don't go at it alone.

3. "Sometimes no matter how well you prepare, or how well you perform, you still [fail]. It's just the way life is sometimes. If you want to change the world, get over [failure] and keep moving forward... You will fail. You will likely fail often. It will be painful. It will be discouraging. At times it will test you to your very core. But if you want to change the world, don't be afraid..." Grit, defined as passion and perseverance for very long-term goals, is said to be one of the most critical success factors for entrepreneurs. Establish a bold vision and don't let anything, especially a little failure, stop you from accomplishing it.

4. "Know that life is not fair and that you will fail often. But if take you

take some risks, step up when the times are toughest, face down the bullies, lift up the downtrodden, and never, ever give up – if you do these things, then the next generation and the generations that follow will live in a world far better than the one we have today."

Oprah Winfrey

1. "It doesn't matter how far you might rise. At some point you are bound to stumble because if you're constantly doing what we do, raising the bar - if you're constantly pushing yourself higher, higher, the law of averages not to mention the Myth of Icarus predicts that you will at some point fall. And when you do I want you to know this, remember this: There is no such thing as failure."

2. "Failure is just life trying to move us in another direction. Now when you're down there in the hole, it looks like failure. So this past year I had to spoon feed those words to myself. And when you're down in the hole, when that moment comes, it's really okay to feel bad for a little while. Give yourself time to mourn what you think you may have lost, but then here's the key, learn from every mistake because every experience, encounter, and particularly your mistakes are there to teach you and force you into being more who you are."

3. "I have to say that the single most important lesson I learned in 25 years talking every single day to people was that there is a common denominator in our human experience. Most of us, I tell you, we don't want to be divided. What we want, the common denominator that I found in every single interview, is we want to be validated. We want to be understood. I have done over 35,000 interviews in my career and as soon as that camera shuts off everyone always turns to me and inevitably in their own way asks this question: 'Was that okay?'"

4. "I know that you all might have a little anxiety now and hesitation about leaving the comfort of college and putting those Harvard credentials to the test. But no matter what challenges or setbacks or disappointments you may encounter along the way, you will find true success and happiness if you have only one goal, there

really is only one, and that is this: to fulfill the highest, most truthful expression of yourself as a human being."

"The spirit of arrogance most definitely makes you shine. It paints a bright red target on your own forehead."

– Criss Jami
Philosopher & Author of *Killosophy*

Arrogance + Entrepreneurship
Chuck Papageorgiou

I frequently talk with young entrepreneurs who approach me for advice or for investment in their company. Every now and then, one strikes me as someone who has good potential but can use a bit of advice on how to improve their chances by altering their behavior, and I have a deep conversation with them about it. Because of their young age I gave them the benefit of the doubt, and instead of just declining the investment offer, I share what I learned from my experience in the military, consulting, corporate career, and the building of multiple companies. That's how I ended up talking with this very smart, young, entrepreneur, whose communications and behavior came across as arrogant to the people he was asking for help, advice, or money.

My advice was perhaps best summed up by something my old boss in the military used to tell me: "The difference between cocky pilots and arrogant pilots? The cocky ones are still alive." It's the same with entrepreneurs. Being cocky is almost a prerequisite for success, especially when we are pushing a new idea, but being arrogant, especially when you have yet to deliver actual results, can be deadly.

And I did, of course, acknowledge there are some arrogant entrepreneurs who do make it. And there are people like Steve Jobs, Bill Gates, Larry Ellison, Elon Musk, and others like them who have earned the right to be arrogant (even though some are still just cocky). But the rest of us mere mortals, and especially this young man, have not earned that right, and in my maybe not-so-humble opinion, even if we do earn that right, being arrogant is still not something to aspire toward.

That was my message to this young man who was suffering from Founderitis – symptoms include hubris and arrogance – a disease that has killed more companies and good ideas than anything else I have encountered over my life so far.

I thought by having this conversation I had done him a great favor.

But then he went to hear a speech by a very well-known investor and author, who by the way got his money from being an early employee of a very famous company and not by being an actual entrepreneur himself, and heard something different. During the Q&A period the young man asked him, "What do you do when people call you arrogant?" And the great man answered, "Ignore them." And based on those two words, the young man decided it was OK to be arrogant. So we had another conversation to add some nuance to the first one.

When someone calls me arrogant, I ask them to elaborate and sincerely listen to the answer. There is a big difference between arrogance of thought and arrogance of behavior, and there is an even bigger difference between being called arrogant because of my thoughts versus because of my behavior.

On most days, I have at least one thought that challenges the status quo and can easily be considered arrogant by many people, and that's before I finish my first cup of coffee. And I am darn proud of that. I can't do what I do as a serial entrepreneur and investor without that attitude, and the companies I advise and entrepreneurs I mentor expect nothing less. That's arrogance of thought, and it's a good thing. Our world would never change without arrogance of thought. That's the kind of arrogance to aspire to. On the other hand, treating executives or investors with many years of experience who have built or run multi-million dollar companies without the respect they deserve is just arrogant behavior. Trying to force other people to think I am smarter than them just because I have a different way of looking at the world or have a new idea or believe my accomplishments are larger than they are is just arrogant.

If I am humble, I shift the focus to my idea and make it the center point so other people can decide for themselves. If I am arrogant, people focus on me and my idea never gets a chance. Arrogant people are more often than not insecure and they feel a need to put others down. Trying to prove other people are stupid does not necessarily make me any smarter. That's not how ideas are sold. Or as a friend of mine says: You can't win an election simply by convincing 49% of the people their ideas are wrong; it's more important to convince 51% of the people your ideas are right.

Entrepreneurs who have arrogance of thought but are not arrogant change the world. The ones who fail to separate the two most often don't.

"Grit is having stamina. Grit is sticking with your future...and working really hard to make that future a reality. Grit is living life like it's a marathon, not a sprint."

– Angela Lee Duckworth
Psychologist

Get Gritty

Caroline Vanevenhoven

When I was twelve, I saved up my money to buy my very first bike, and when the delivery day finally arrived, I waited for an entire afternoon for my dad to come home so we could go to the store to pick up the item of my dreams. After what was an unnaturally long time bordering on eternity, we finally got to the store. To my shock and horror, when the manager came from the warehouse I did not see my beautiful blue ten-speed (nor did I hear the expected accompaniment of angel's song). Instead I was staring at a heartless, soulless, brown cardboard box – my bike came unassembled.

We brought it home, and I expected to be feeling totally free, hair blowing in the wind, in just a few hours. But then the unexpected occurred, and my dreams of sweet, ten-speed freedom came screeching to a halt the next day when my dad promptly left for a month-long Army Reserve training camp. There sat my unholy cardboard box of dreams. How did we get here? My original goal was to ride my bike. I didn't set a goal to prove I had patience, to prove I could work to save money, or that I could build a bike. My goal was to ride my brand new blue bike as fast as I was able, and now there were all these unexpected challenges in my way and I didn't know the first thing about assembling bicycles!

Thankfully I didn't know what I didn't know, so I did the first thing that came to mind: I got out my dad's tools, unpacked the bike parts (there were so many they nearly covered the entire driveway), and began to assemble the bike myself with no help or oversight. I was driven. I was committed. I persevered on with reckless abandon, as I was way too stubborn to quit. I can't remember now how long it actually took me, but by the next day the bike was together and ready to ride.

Sometimes you don't know what you can't do, and you just do it anyway. Occasionally it's because you have to, and occasionally it's because you don't know you're not qualified. I didn't compile any data on the success rate of individual pre-teen bike assembly. I didn't poll my neighbors to see if it was a good idea to assemble the bike alone. I didn't write a plan, set goals, list strategic milestones, or go out and buy a new set of tools for the project. I didn't wait for the perfect day, or time, or weather conditions. I knew I wanted to ride my new bike, and my gut said, "Do it," so I listened.

While most of us would not choose to go back to our awkward pre-teen years, imagine what would happen if, as adults, we still maintained the same "anything is possible" mindset we had at age twelve. My twelve-year-old self did not have mechanical smarts, and I had virtually no experience using wrenches, screwdrivers, nuts, and bolts. But, what I lacked in experience I made up for in stamina and determination. What would the world look like with less skepticism and more willing suspension of disbelief? Children are energy-fueled whirling dervishes of commotion. They do not run their lives like sprints; rather they run them like marathons. They are sponges that thirst for stimulation, information, and experiences during much of their waking minutes. They use their stamina and determination to keep growing.

Take that sort of mentality to heart. There are researchers who argue that talent alone does not make a person successful. In her TED Talk on grit, Angela Lee Duckworth summarized her research on predicting success in adults and children, in which she found that intelligence and talent were not good predictors of success. That's correct. Being smart and gifted is not enough. The successful managers, CEOs, spelling bee contestants, West Point cadets, and brand new teachers she studied had a marathon mentality. They had passion and perseverance for very long-term goals. They had grit!

It all sounds so easy, but if getting gritty was as easy as it sounds, then why aren't we all terribly successful and accomplished? Duckworth argues that "Achievement = Talent x Effort," and that while talent is important, effort is also requisite. (Innate talent aside, you can't force someone to put forth more effort, so the real trick becomes figuring out why some of us persevere through difficult tasks while others simply quit.) The answer may lie in K. Anders Ericsson's work on deliberate practice. Ericsson argues there are four prerequisites to deliberate practice: setting a specific stretch goal, focusing on a single task, getting immediate and informative feedback, and practicing repeatedly until you hit fluency.

I think we can now start to really see all the pieces of the puzzle. Refer back to the early definition of grit provided (viz., passion and perseverance for very long term goals), then recognize that deliberate practice is often both time-consuming and not fun. Often the things we want are difficult to achieve, requiring a lot of work and not always a lot of excitement. This is where passion comes into play. Be passionate about your idea. It's not enough to like it or the vision of what it will become. You've got to totally love it, so much so that you're willing to put in the effort.

Set both long-term and short-term goals.

It is important to have a big picture vision of the goal you are working toward as well as a realistic timeline for that goal. But you also need to set tangible short-term goals, or milestones to hit along the journey, to keep yourself from becoming overwhelmed. Be they daily, weekly, or monthly, make your short-term goals visible. Write them down. Tell someone who will help keep you accountable. Keep a journal. If you don't know how best to set, measure, and achieve goals, there are entire self-help sections of books dedicated to that subject, so hop online and find the one that most resonates with your style and personality.

Redefine the word failure.

Failure is not a permanent condition unless you make it so. I'm sure you've heard by now that it is important to learn from your mistakes. You'll hear it echoed in this book as well, though perhaps I'll frame it a bit differently here. Change your mindset about failure. Change your definition of failure. Heck, go so far as to take it out of your vocabulary entirely. Remove all negative connotations of failure except those that fire you up to work harder the next time. View failure as a positive - an opportunity to learn from what did not work so you can figure out what will work next time.

Don't stop, grow.

Look for opportunities to learn from anything and anyone. Adopt what Stanford University psychologist Carol Dweck calls a growth mindset, which is the idea that we can purposely expand our capacity to learn and solve problems. Use your talents and smarts as your foundation and then build on that foundation by learning, experiencing, and doing. Be dynamic, never static. Believe that as your experiences grow, so do your intelligence and talent.

Now go get gritty...

"Success is most often achieved by those who don't know that failure is inevitable."

– Coco Chanel
Entrepreneur and one of *Time*'s
100 Most Influential People of the 20th Century

Become Rejection Proof
Eric Liguori

As every male college student is aware, rejection happens! Becoming accustomed to rejection takes practice, and learning how to overcome and harness rejection is critical for success. For this reason, I often suggest entrepreneurs formally undergo "rejection therapy," a phrase originally coined by Jason Comely. Rejection therapy is pretty much what it sounds like: You intentionally seek out rejection over and over again until you are immune from the pain of hearing the word "no."

To help in the quest to become rejection proof, Betsy Hays, Connor Alstrom, and I developed a series of entrepreneur-specific rejection therapy action items when we created the Entrepreneurship Action Deck (available on Amazon). I've used these items in class with some success, so I recommend giving them a try. Below are a few of my favorites:

Rejection Therapy Prompt #1: Head down to your local newspaper or news station and ask to speak to a reporter. Pitch your business.

It's too easy to email or fax a press release to a news desk. You've got to get your hands dirty. Show up, preferably not during a prime news time (although that would definitely ensure you get rejected), and make your pitch. The worst they can say is "no," and "no" is exactly what we want to happen. Get used to "no," start understanding why you received a "no," and then begin to work at developing the skill of converting that "no" into a "not now" or a "yes."

Rejection Therapy Prompt #2: Get a $20 bill, head to a coffee shop, and randomly offer to buy other customers coffee in exchange for feedback on your latest idea.

I adapted this "$20 Starbucks Test" from Sean Johnson's blog at snootymonkey.com. It's one of my favorite exercises because, when done correctly, it's a two-for-one deal: You get rejected and you get some great, candid feedback on early stage ideas. (Hint: For even more candid feedback, lie and say it's a friend's idea, and be sure to note that you yourself have mixed feelings about it.) Before you call me crazy for suggesting this, note that Ben Silbermann, founder of Pinterest, once said he randomly approached strangers in Palo Alto coffee shops to get feedback on the early Pinterest platform.

Rejection Therapy Prompt #3: Request a face-to-face meeting with your dream mentor.

A student of mine recently landed an interview with Jeff Vinik, owner of the Tampa Bay Lightning and the entrepreneur behind a multi-billion dollar redevelopment project in downtown Tampa, as a result of this exercise. How did he do it you wonder? He found Vinik's administrative assistant's email address online, emailed her, and played the student card. I've also had students land internships as a result of this rejection prompt. Neither of these outcomes are technically what we're going for here (no rejection occurred), but they're about as good of an unintended outcome as one could hope for.

Now let's take this up a notch…

If you want to really develop a rejection-proof mindset, you need look no further than the story of Jia Jiang. Jiang had a paralyzing fear of failure. As he himself stated, "I hate being judged and rejected in a business setting, whether it's being turned down when making a sale or getting blasted after a pitch. I hate it!"

To combat his fear, Jiang set out to undergo 100 Days of Rejection. Each day he created a new opportunity to experience rejection. One day he approached a stranger and asked to borrow $100. Another day he rang a doorbell and inquired whether he could play soccer in that person's backyard. (He got a yes on this one.) And on yet another day, he boarded a Southwest Airlines flight and asked the flight attendant if he could give the safety announcement. (The attendant said no but did agree to let him give the opening welcome message.) To make it for a full 100 days, he had to get creative: fix a PC at the Apple Store, sell cookies for the Girl Scouts, ask if he could sleep in a Mattress Firm store, get a private jet ride from Tony Hsieh, give a college lecture, and be a tour guide at a museum.

Some days Jiang was successful, and on others he failed gloriously. In either case, he experienced and overcame the fear of failure. Moreover, he learned rejection often was a reflection of the rejector more than himself. Jiang's lessons reveal the necessity of shifting how we view rejection: It is an opinion, nothing more. Don't let one random person's (or one mentor's, or one friend's, or one professor's…) judgment of your ideas stop you; you're stronger and more perseverant than that.

As you consider formulating your own rejection therapy plan, note Jiang had three rules governing the rejection opportunities he pursued: It must be ethical, it must be legal, and it can't defy the laws of physics. He also suggests some additional tips you may want to consider while putting together your plan:

1. Have a predetermined number of rejection opportunities you will pursue and don't stop until you hit that number.
2. Have a good reason as to why you are making your ask so people don't think you are entirely crazy.
3. Exude confidence.
4. When someone says "no," consider that an invititation to negotiate and ask what you can do to convert that "no" to a "yes."

In closing, take a minute to self-assess and self-reflect. Do you seek out rejection, or do you avoid situations where rejection could occur at all costs? Does rejection roll off of your shoulders like it's nothing, or does it feel like a sucker punch to the face? Reflecting back on his rejection therapy experience, Jiang notes that "by challenging [him]self to seek out rejection again and again, [he] came to see rejection – and even the world around [him] – very differently."

"I shall either find a way or make one."

– Hannibal
Punic Carthaginian Military Commander, circa 221 BC

Beer, Sex, and Bricolage

Jeff Vanevenhoven

While it's safe to say the majority of college students are familiar with the first two terms in the title, the same may not apply to the third. Bricolage is the process of actively solving problems and/or seeking opportunities by creatively repurposing the resources that are already available to you; in other words, it's making do with whatever is at hand to accomplish your goals. Things still a little fuzzy? Here are two stories of successful student entrepreneurs that will hopefully help you better understand the concept of bricolage and how impactful it can be.

Need Beer? Henry's Story...

Let's begin with the creative mind of one Henry Schwarz. Henry and his friends were hardworking and industrious but also thirsty and broke – the stereotypical college dilemma. Looking for a solution, Henry and his friends turned their love of hops and barley into a home brewing pastime. A number of friends and acquaintances soon took interest and began to suggest styles and flavors, which got Henry thinking: What if there was a way to harness the power of "the mob" and build a company upon the ideas of these early customers? Shortly thereafter, Henry's notions were confirmed when he read a case study on a Chicago-based T-shirt company that used customer submissions and crowd-sourced voting to print exactly what people wanted.

With the guidance and support of the University of Wisconsin-Whitewater's student incubator, Henry and his partners launched Mobcraft, the world's first completely crowdsourced brewery, in 2012. Like the Chicago T-shirt company, the Mobcraft master brewers collect recipes and ideas from the public before narrowing submissions down to the best 4-5 to be voted upon by customers and followers. Each vote constitutes as a preorder, and at the close of voting, Mobcraft knows exactly what "the mob" wants as well as exactly the number of orders to be filled.

In the beginning, Henry and his partners kept overhead and production costs low by brewing in the vacant tanks of local breweries and working out of the incubator. Their brews quickly began winning awards, both locally in Wisconsin and nationally in Colorado, at which point Henry began lobbying for changes in state legislation to allow for the crowdfunding of companies. He succeeded, subsequently raising two rounds of funding while also opening the door for future companies to benefit from crowdfunding.

Need Dates? Joe's Story...

Joe Scanlin's story is a great example of the benefits of redeploying resources in novel ways. It begins with Joe and his friends hoping to narrow the dating playing field to make things easier on themselves. Was there some way to measure which pub, bar, or club had the greatest concentration of eligible singles?

As Joe began to explore this idea, he started to wonder what else he might measure, and eventually he landed on the use of imprints to discern how long someone stays in front of a product or display. Measurement of that type had many possible applications for retail, restaurants, bars, and convention spaces. As he further progressed down this path, he found that his well-developed network of senior executives cultivated from his prior work in the business world and through networking events and social connections became an invaluable resource for him, especially in terms of customer discovery.

Once he validated and narrowed down his ideas, Joe dove right into the engineering of the pressure mats he would use to measure how long a person remained at a particular place. Seeking inspiration, he tore apart one of the popular video game mats commonly used in dance games. And while this is a perfect example of resource recombination and improvisation, it is worth noting Joe's friend was not too happy about Joe using their dance mat for prototyping.

Justifiably angry friend aside, Joe was now able to begin testing what it would take to measure where people were standing and for how long. He worked with aspiring engineers from across campus to develop prototype iterations, some as class projects and others as side jobs. Using these prototypes, he was able to demonstrate enough proof of concept to convince a local company to invest in creating a working test module/lab/study for use on convention floors.

While working on his prototypes, Joe was able to continue to grow his prospect market to a point that allowed him to stream real-time predictive analytics upon going live with his first proof of concept. This advancement ultimately led to Joe's series A round of funding. Since then, Joe's Scanalytics Incorporated has won the People's Choice Internet of Things Award two years in a row and has just moved into his second new office space in an awesome and highly coveted Milwaukee building.

The Importance of Bricolage in Student Startups

Most of the students I've worked with are in the early stages of their journey into entrepreneurship. If we generalize the entrepreneurial process as evolution through identification, validation, development, and exploitation of opportunities, most students will often start with trying to identify opportunities and validate demand. As anyone that has navigated the process knows, resource constraints can happen in each (or all) of these stages, illustrating that entrepreneurship is part trial and error, part creativity, and part serendipity. If we are to excel in this environment we need to train ourselves to think differently; to think about how we can leverage the resources and relationships that are already within reach rather than trying to acquire new resources we think we need based on some plan.

As Karl Weick notes, entrepreneurs must have an intimate knowledge of their available resources and be aware and observant of their environment to successfully use bricolage in the entrepreneurial process. Think of your networks as resources to be exploited and constantly monitor your environment for new opportunities. Additionally, look to your community for support and try to understand how businesses similar to yours operate so you can identify opportunities for partnership and/or instances in which you could leverage their excess capacity to your advantage.

In their most recent book, Heidi Neck and colleagues suggest we can teach ourselves to think this way in terms of creation with existing resources. One great example from this book is a mental exercise created by Andrew Corbett and Candida Brush that asks you to list your five most significant personal accomplishments and rank them from one (most significant) to five (least significant) in order of their significance to you.

Next, take some time to think about these accomplishments and write down the knowledge, skills, and abilities (KSAs) you had to use to make the accomplishment a reality. Once you finish making that list, reflect back on all five and circle the KSAs you believe were most influential to your success. In an only a short period of time you will begin to see themes emerge; perhaps you have social media expertise, or leadership skills, or are a strong project manager.

Now think about your team and have them work through the same activity. Are there common themes you all share? If so, can you build a business from the areas in which you are cumulatively very strong? The key take away here is that anyone can develop or create something they are proud of and enjoy doing simply by starting with their means: who you are and what and who you know. It's all about awareness and self-understanding.

The struggles seen in Henry's and Joe's stories are not unique; uncertainty threatens to cripple many student startups. Thankfully, both Henry and Joe ended up being positive examples of how bricolage can help successfully manage dynamic, ad hoc situations. The formula here is simple: Know yourself, make do with available resources, refuse to be constrained by limitations, and improvise as needed. If you can do this, the things you can accomplish are limitless. Who knows, you may even get a date or at least a cold beer.

"The person who has not travelled widely thinks his or her mother
is the only cook."

– East African Proverb

Backpack Entrepreneurship
Aris Creates & Stephen Hnilica

There is a growing movement of people who want to live and work by their own rules. More and more entrepreneurs, technologists, and workers in general are seeking location-independent lifestyles that foster and support environments for creative productivity, the building of businesses, and balance. Industry disruptions, websites, mobile applications, smart phones, tablets, the Internet of things, couch surfing, and Airbnb are the objective phenomena empowering the creation of location-independent backpack entrepreneurs. Technology and improved global infrastructure now allow us to communicate, work, and travel more quickly, inexpensively, and easily than ever before. So in January 2016, we launched the Backpack Entrepreneurs website and podcast and departed the U.S. with a goal of working remotely and traveling the world.

One can define "backpack entrepreneur" in many ways. Perhaps it's the person who floats around the U.S. doing odd freelance jobs from his laptop with no real commitments or responsibilities. Perhaps it's the person who detaches herself from possessions, owning only a backpack with some clothes and the bare equipment necessary to do her job. Or perhaps you adopt the definition we've adopted: traveling entrepreneurs exploring the world and making an impact. For us this is not a "trip"; it's a mindset and a lifestyle, a way of both living and working. We view this as an opportunity to create a life that blends into as well as complements our entrepreneurial, social, and leisure activities.

Our journey started in late 2015. We formulated a vague plan and channeled all our ambition into making this a reality. We considered all the resources we had at our disposal: prior personal and business experience; social connections; lots of web and app-based tools to make things like travel, communicating, and connecting easier; and our lofty belief that we could make this happen if we put our minds to it. For us, traveling is a big part of creating the environment necessary for learning, growth, and creativity. Both of us get a bit restless and bored by the same old stimuli. You won't find too much novelty by remaining in the same place for any length of time. So traveling, which exponentially increases our chances to experience new things, is key to keeping creative energy flowing.

Aside from stimulating and fueling creative energy, there are many other benefits to our backpack entrepreneur mindset and lifestyle. We only take on customers that support our approach, staying away from those who put up barriers and try to overly control how, when, and where we work. We strive to be our own bosses responsible for our own financial well-being. We set our schedules not only to accomplish the work that needs to be done, but also to suit our work and lifestyle preferences, thus prompting higher levels of productivity. And as a bonus, we get to curate our experiences within the places we travel, which gives us larger and more diverse perspectives on the intersection of art, culture, science, business, and public policy.

Being a backpack entrepreneur is not without challenges, however. Securing work visas internationally can be a complicated process because the definition of "work" varies by country and because our traveling concept of work is a relatively new phenomenon not well defined in current laws. While it is easy and relatively harmless to simply claim to be on vacation, it's also risky. If you are exposed as having done anything defined as work without a proper work visa, you could be fined, jailed, and even lose the privilege to re-enter that country indefinitely. Some countries, such as the United Kingdom, would consider this seemingly harmless white lie a very serious offense, so tread carefully and err on the side of compliance.

Budgeting is another major concern for backpack entrepreneurs. You must find a realistic way to live and budget just as you would in your hometown with a job and a steady paycheck. If you fail to budget appropriately, your funds may not last until the end of your journey, and finding a quick job to hold you over is much more difficult (if not impossible) when traveling internationally. Remember: Prices and demand change from location to location, so your budget must reflect that volatility. Plan to the best of your ability, but have a contingency fund.

Lastly, finding reliable high-speed Internet access is often difficult. Many locales are simply not the technology hotspots we've become accustomed to, so it's important to be prepared to make trade-offs and get creative with how you prioritize and accomplish your work. Despite our best efforts, we've spent many days faced with poor connectivity and no choice but to make the best of an inconvenient situation.

There is no specific set of hard skills required for backpack entrepreneurs. Instead, successful backpack entrepreneurs share a common mindset that governs the way they approach their work and their lives. For example, backpack entrepreneurs are flexible and understand that delegating skill-intensive tasks to qualified freelancers is often more efficient and productive than completing the work themselves.

Below is a list of four additional traits common among prospective backpack entrepreneurs:

#1. Ability to Zone Out

You must be able to zone out from what's going on around you and focus on the task at hand. Remember, you're not a tourist; you're a backpack entrepreneur. You've got your company, your customers, and your responsibilities to attend to. Most of us who are building, running, and growing our businesses need to create uninterrupted periods of time that allow for deep focus and working our asses off. Work time, like play time, is sacred.

#2. Knowing When to Cut the Fat

Knowing when and where to cut the fat is another requirement for any type of entrepreneur, backpacker or not. I don't mean getting six-pack abs, either; I'm talking about getting rid of all that is unnecessary. Sleeping in a new city every week is much more difficult when you're lugging around six suitcases. You don't need a day planner, calculator, atlas, and flashlight when you've got a smartphone in your pocket, and similarly, you don't need five pairs of dress shoes or ten pairs of dress pants to authentically connect with the world around you.

To cut the fat, you first need to mentally accept that all you really need are the bare necessities for operating your business and living your life. Once that's done, evaluate your belongings to identify those things that are truly critical to attaining your goals and get rid of everything else. You're living a lifestyle that may require you to change your entire business model overnight; holding onto extraneous assets or processes is only going to slow you down in your most critical moments.

#3. Working and Playing Hard

As entrepreneurs we often work incredibly hard for very long periods of time to get the job done, sometimes in upwards of 80 hours a week. While these long hours are often necessary, it is important you train yourself to recognize when its time for a break. Travel is likely the primary reason why you chose to be a backpack entrepreneur in the first place, so make sure you leave time to enjoy the benefits your new lifestyle allows. The ability to visit Buckingham Palace while you're in London, to go on a hike down the Spanish coast, or to have a meal without your laptop in front of you is part of your end goal. Work hard, play hard, and protect your balance.

#4. Ignoring the Haters

There will be customers who don't like your nomadic approach to business; ignore them and focus on the customers who understand and support your goals instead. Similarly, your friends and family will likely need some convincing before they fully accept your unconventional take on work and life, so be prepared to show them why the backpack entrepreneur lifestyle is not only financially viable, but also something that makes you happy.

If you're one of the thousands of people considering the backpack entrepreneur's journey, we hope we've been able to shed some light on the things that helped us make it happen. For more advice and insight, check out our Backpack Entrepreneurs podcast in which we share our journey as we travel from place to place, discussing our experiences, successes, failures, and entrepreneurial observations. Most importantly, however, remember that attitude determines aptitude and that the little things will fall into place if you approach them with the right mindset.

I read an interesting article by Jay Meistrich about a year ago in which he relayed his experience of working 50-hour weeks, living out of only a 40-liter backpack, and traveling to 45 cities across 20 countries while launching his company Moo.do. In the article, Meistrich made a compelling case for his nomad lifestyle. To begin, he saved thousands in cost of living expenses, with his average monthly total being only $2,921 while abroad versus nearly $6,000 in San Francisco and $4,700 in Seattle. Furthermore, living as a nomad increased his productivity and expanded his understanding of different cultures.

After reading Meistrich's article, I saw Aris and Stephen present their backpack entrepreneurship concept at a community event in late 2015 and immediately knew I wanted to include an entry on their story in this book. While it may not be for everyone, I think their journey does a great job of illustrating the need to constantly challenge the assumptions (e.g., it's too expensive to travel) that keep us from discarding our everyday routines in favor of a new and potentially enriching way of doing things. Pictured below are Aris and Stephen working remotely from a coffee shop in Bath, UK.

Part 3

Succeeding as a Student Entrepreneur

"Intensity begets greatness."

– Seal
Four-Time Grammy Award Winner

Six Questions to Answer Before Starting Up
Michael Luchies

If there's one thing I know about launching a startup on campus, it's how to drive a business right into the ground. I'm far from the only one, as approximately 90% of tech startups fail. When taking into consideration all of the college startups that don't even set up their legal structure, there's reason to believe the failure rate is closer to 95-99%. Of those that don't fail, most will go on to be stable small businesses. Very few will ever grace the pages of *Entrepreneur* or launch an IPO.

Tasting failure is a likely part of every entrepreneur's journey, but being an entrepreneur is about beating the odds – and that's the attitude you need to have to make it.

Looking back on all of my early ventures, there were obvious truths that I didn't want to accept. Because I failed in one of the areas below or another, so did my businesses. Give your startup every chance at success by knowing potential risks, preparing and researching, and asking yourself the following six questions.

1. Why hasn't this been done before?

If your answer to "Why hasn't this been done before?" is "because no one has ever thought of it," you're wrong. Ideas are a dime a dozen, and while you're protecting your idea in hopes of it becoming huge, there are five other entrepreneurs working on the same exact idea.

In 2012 I had an idea just crazy enough to work. After a game of pool, I came up with the thought of playing pool with your feet, soccer-like balls, and a small grass court. I shared my idea for "KickPool" with friends and co-workers, and they all thought I was crazy. I didn't lose hope for my idea, but I waited...and waited.

In November of 2014, I nearly threw my computer against the wall at a Starbucks. I had visited ESPN.com and saw a link to a video about a brand new sport sweeping the world. The game was called Snookball. It was created by a couple of French entrepreneurs, and it was nearly identical to my concept for the game. I failed to act on what I thought was a good idea while others worked on it halfway across the world.

Ideas aren't rare or unique – executing well is.

Take an honest and deep look into your idea to find out why this hasn't been done before. Does no one else have the specific skillset or team to pull it off, is it a bad idea, is someone working on it right now, or is the market not ready for it yet? There are many possibilities, but finding reasons why this doesn't exist or why someone isn't doing this properly can save you time and money or help you discover where others, including myself, went wrong and how you can avoid their mistakes.

2. Do I need additional capital, or can the business compete and survive bootstrapped?

There is an odd fascination in the startup world with investments. A large investment is praised like a source of pride and achievement, but many founders are jumping to raise money before properly analyzing whether they actually need it or not. Not all startups need an investment to get going.

Make no mistake about getting an investment in your startup – you're acquiring debt. Raise away if it's vital to your business, but the longer you can wait and the more you can build your business without investment, the better. Also, remember that taking on investment is bringing investors' egos and ideas and added pressure to succeed into your startup as well. Make sure you're prepared for the challenge. Waiting until your business has established a foothold in the marketplace and a higher valuation will lower the amount of equity you need to give away and increase the interest in your business and the number of investment options you'll have.

While raising rounds of funding for your business has its risks and considerations, so does the decision to bootstrap – starting up on an extremely limited budget. Many startups can't start or survive for long bootstrapped. If you plan to build the next Twitter or Facebook, it could be 10 years before you bring in enough revenue to pay employees, but you certainly can't wait that long to bring in talent to help build the business. If deciding to bootstrap, earning revenue as quickly as possible will need to be a priority, and it may force you to rush the development process, which is what will likely determine your startup's success or failure.

Whatever you decide to do, research all the available options for your company. If you do decide to go after investments, make sure to work vigorously on your business while seeking capital. If your heart is truly in the business, you'll find a way. Create strategic partnerships, work a part-time job for the capital you need, apply for business plan competitions – just don't sit on your idea waiting for something to fall in your lap.

3. Are you the best person to bring this to market?

I'm confident in my ability as a young entrepreneur, but if Twitter, Facebook, or Snapchat would've been my ideas, these companies would not exist today, at least not because of me. Think about it. Can you name one extremely successful business that succeeded with a great idea without a dynamic founder and/or a strong team? Are you willing to work hard enough to become the best person to bring your idea to the market?

If your business relies on technology, a website, an app, or anything related to the Internet, wearables, the smart home, or a related field – are you a developer or engineer? If not, do you have a technical co-founder? If the answer is no, you aren't the right person to start this business. Let that sink in. Now suck it up and either make yourself the best person to build this business or start something else.

4. What if your idea does not become a huge success? Is it still something you want to pursue?

When interviewing Upstart Co-Founder Paul Gu, who dropped out of Yale to pursue a Theil Fellowship, he stressed the importance of not going after an idea just because you think it could eventually become a big business. Paul said to ask yourself, "If this weren't going to be a big and successful business, would it still be interesting to me to work on this?"

Most young entrepreneurs, even wildly successful ones, rarely build multi-billion dollar businesses, or even multi-million dollar businesses. You can have a fantastic life running a strong small business, but if your goal is to build an empire, you're not starting up for the right reason. I've been a part of several startups where our sole goal was to build a massive business worth millions. While I truly believe it's possible, it's not probable, and I'm about 0-for-10 when using this strategy.

Is your venture or idea exciting enough to spend the next few years of your life on? Will there be no other idea or venture that will be able to distract you from creating this in the near future? If you answered no or maybe to either of the previous two questions, you may need to take a step back and rethink if this is really something you want to pursue. Life is short, so chase things you love, not just things you think could be big.

5. Who's with me?

No individual man or woman can build an empire alone. Successful entrepreneurs surround themselves with amazing, talented people who can help them build their business. Having a strong co-founder or founding team can increase your ability to get things done and help recruit additional help. Who is on your side and willing to build this business with you? If you're not getting any support, is it because people don't believe in you, the business, or something else? Leaders need to be visionaries to get other people to believe in them.

I failed to get people involved in my early ventures because I was either not willing to recruit or too stingy with equity to bring anyone qualified onto my team.

6. The most important question of them all: What do you really want to accomplish?

Why do we want to be entrepreneurs anyway? I used to think I wanted to build a multi-billion dollar business and be on the cover of *Entrepreneur*. It wasn't until years later that I took a step back and thought about my 80-year-old self and what I would be proud of looking back on when it came to my life. Turns out, I didn't care about the money or the fame. I cared about helping entrepreneurs solve problems and grow their businesses.

Ask yourself what you want to do with your life and what drives you, and then make sure any business venture, job, spouse, or commitment aligns with that end goal.

Don't ignore these questions or signs that your startup may or may not be the right business for you to start. Do your research, surround yourself with amazing people, stay true to your passion, and follow your heart – and even if you fail, you'll succeed.

"There is no better than adversity. Every defeat, every heartbreak, every loss contains its own seed, its own lesson on how to improve your performance the next time."

– Malcolm X
Civil Rights Activist

From Nothing to Great
Daniel James Scott

Let's talk Billy Joel, Stephen Sondheim, and Kevin Systrom.

Billy Joel

Did you know that it took Billy Joel 20 years from his first piano lesson before he started his ascent toward becoming the sixth best-selling recording artist in US history? 20 whole years.

Billy's mother encouraged him to play the piano because his father was a concert pianist. When Joel was 8, his parents divorced, and his dad moved to Vienna. With his father now gone, Billy's interests shifted toward boxing. After 22 wins in the ring, a broken nose forced him to focus once more on music, at which point he began playing in bars to help his mother make ends meet.

A skill borne and nurtured mostly out of necessity turned into a compulsion after Joel saw the Beatles perform on Ed Sullivan. "I'm going to be in a band," Billy told himself. After 12 years of tickling the ivories in relative anonymity, Joel spent the next eight years in the music industry, releasing four albums with three different bands.

Eventually Joel released his first solo record, and shortly thereafter his label owner, Artie Ripp, sold Joel's contract to Columbia Records. Under Columbia's guidance, Billy released his second and seminal solo album The Pianoman, which was named after a song he'd written for his regular bar patrons. The tour that followed cemented Billy's spot at the top of his field, more than 20 years after he'd first sat down on the piano bench.

Stephen Sondheim

Stephen Sondheim wrote his first musical, *By George*, at the age of 15. His mentor, Oscar Hammerstein II, called it the worst thing he'd ever seen. A string of 10 straight unsuccessful musicals followed, and at age 24, Sondheim remained unknown. But then, at age 25, he finally made magic with *West Side Story*, at which point he began his unprecedented rise to become what The New York Times calls the "greatest and perhaps best-known artist in American musical theater."

By the time I discovered Sondheim's work in 1990, he was 50 years old. At that point, he'd spent half of his life as a nobody and half as a legend. In the 25 years that followed West Side Story, he won six Grammys, six Tonys, six Drama Desk Awards, three Laurence Olivier Awards, an Academy Award, a Pulitzer Prize in Drama, and had convinced a young Jonathan Larson to write what would become the international phenomenon *Rent*.

Good thing he didn't quit at 24.

Kevin Systrom

Kevin Systrom didn't discover coding until high school. When he was finally bitten by the bug (pardon my pun), he left his home in Massachusetts and traversed the country to attend college at Stanford. During college, he was accepted into the Mayfield Fellows Program for high-tech entrepreneurs and also interned at Odeo, where he witnessed their pivot to Twitter firsthand. That was a lesson he'd never forget.

After college, Kevin took a job as a Marketing Manager at Google but left after only two years to join a group of former co-workers at Nextstep. Nextstep was quickly acquired by Facebook, but not before Kevin had the idea to merge Nextstep's location check-in capabilities with the burgeoning social gaming movement. He pitched his idea to a couple of venture capitalists at party and secured $500,000 to start Burbn. Burbn didn't take off, but thankfully Kevin remembered Odeo's pivot to Twitter and—10 months after starting his business—he launched Instagram. A year later, he sold to Facebook for $1 billion.

The stories of Billy Joel, Stephen Sondheim, Kevin Systrom, and many others I didn't mention here all follow a similar pattern that starts with a long, hard period of thankless work, tireless dedication, and relative obscurity... and ends in a win. None of these folks are supernatural. They're just regular people who prioritized their passions and refused to give up, even amid failure. They kept fighting until the right opportunity arose and they eventually won. Which brings me to you, our newest crop of entrepreneurs.

You are the future of this great country. We need you to win.

But how you ask? Well, we're often told that our attitude defines our ability to succeed. Be smart and humble, they tell us. As if smart is an optional setting. Oh, and remind me again, is Brian Williams the humble one, or is that Mark Cuban? Yeah, that's what I thought.

If it's not just smarts and humility, then what is it? Silicon Valley "gurus" tell us that winning comes from failing fast and often, iterating and pivoting. Yet even with this advice, we still haven't quite mastered the fine art of building successful companies. Startups are just as speculative today as they were ten years ago, and seed stage investing is no easier now than before all the fancy analytics and tricks.

With all these methods, frameworks, and platforms, you'd think we have this figured out. But we don't. The thing is, startups work when markets explode from seemingly nowhere and you have a product that meets this new market's need. Skrillex fronted a post-hardcore band at what appeared to be the wrong time, but he broke through as a DJ at the exact perfect right time to lead an EDM revolution.

The lesson here is that you simply cannot analyze, fail, and iterate your way to explosive market growth. Life is measured on wins and results, not attempts and attitude. Our brains play tricks on us. We think, "If I get lucky, I'll find something I want to do, and it will become my passion…my life's work." But starting with luck puts your chances of winning in life about the same as in the lottery: depressingly tiny.

Real winners think the opposite way. They don't wait for luck to get started. Instead, they jump right in, identify their passions, and toil away at them, waiting years if not decades to trigger a desire and a little bit of luck that they can eventually leverage into something much bigger.

Just doing something requires absolutely zero buy in. Doing stuff is easy. Working at your passion, however, requires dedication, resiliency, and execution. You can fake a smile, but you can't fake passion. It's a compulsion. It's putting in your 10,000 hours of practice unnoticed while everyone else folds to their most recent desires. Effort for the sake of effort with no complaints and no whining. Confidence in yourself without ego.

Cementing and pursuing your passion is harder than anything you could ever imagine, and it often offers no external rewards. I mention this because every successful founder starts the same way. For Billy Joel, it took 20 years. Sondheim took 25, and Systrom over a decade. Amazon and Apple operated without generating a profit for seven years and are now the titans of technology. All of these stories help us understand the steps for how innovators win and take a market seemingly overnight.

To help me explain further, I'd like to share with you the path to market of Barefoot Wine. Founders Michael Houlihan and Bonnie Harvey couldn't compete in major retail initially, so they played to their strengths and focused on small, local charity events where Barefoot could support the same cause as the attendees. From these events they created an invaluable, instant connection with their customers that would have taken millions of dollars to build otherwise.

The charity event attendees saw Barefoot as a brand that cares about what they care about, and from this Michael and Bonnie created advocates, known as early adopters, in markets all over the country. In addition, the charity events helped support Barefoot's local retail efforts, allowing Michael and Bonnie the leverage needed to eventually build out the early majority market through major retail.

Barefoot was a serious wine, consistently winning medals at major tastings, yet it maintained an image that was laid-back, casual, and approachable. It was made to be a wine for everyone, not just serious wine drinkers. Keeping with this relaxed theme, Michael and Bonnie sold to retailers in vacation towns where there were smaller stores and fewer big names. In places like these, Barefoot could stand out. And because visitors were on vacation, they were more willing to try something new. Barefoot also sold through stores and restaurants on military bases. The bases were willing to try out new brands, and the Barefoot's casual, beachy image resonated with soldiers stuck on base who longer for a taste of California magic.

Barefoot took the pursuit of their founders' passion, along with a game changer in the form of shared charitable pursuits, and turned luck into leverage. And they did it with almost no money in a non-traditional way, forgoing the "normal" path just like Joel, Sondheim, and Systrom. And you can do it too, no matter where you are, with very little capital and a big helping of hard work.

"Make a choice about what's important and let everything else go."

– Peter Coughter
Author, *The Art of the Pitch*

90 Seconds of Fame (aka Your 90-Second Pitch)
Daniel McDonald

Let's discuss the elevator pitch, otherwise known as the art of being able to concisely and convincingly convey enough information to peak the interest of investors in short, and often spontaneous, circumstances. Learning to effectively construct and deliver a pitch is a critical skill for the modern day entrepreneur. For students, a good pitch is often your first means of establishing your legitimacy to a prospect, and it's likely also a required component of almost any entrepreneurship class you will take. Pitch competitions are prevalent nationally, regionally, and locally, and they often offer cash prizes. Savvy students participate in these competitions to gain not just bootstrapped capital, but also exposure, mentorship, and feedback.

I have seen many pitch successes and equally as many pitch failures. Those that stand out as the winners share common attributes, and those that tank often do so because they failed to follow some simple pitch fundamentals. What follows is a universal 90-second pitch platform I use when working with anyone preparing to pitch.

The Four Questions

First, understand that content is key. There is no substitute for high quality content. Assuming you have a great idea and/or business model to pitch, then the pitch itself really becomes all about two factors: (1) the delivery and (2) your ability to effectively respond to the questions that follow. To adequately cover your bases, there are four key questions you need to answer prior to delivering your pitch:

1. What is the problem?

In any pitch, it is critical that you clearly communicate the problem you are addressing. Convince the investor that this problem is important to potential consumers and that solving it will be revenue generating. In addition, make sure the investor knows who experiences the problem and how big the audience for your idea really is. Simplicity is a powerful tool in pitches, so keep your problem statement limited to one sentence.

2. What is the solution?

Once you have clearly stated the problem, you need to explain your proposed solution. Your pitch will need to be adaptable to a variety of different audiences, so be sure to avoid jargon or industry lingo unless you are 100% confident all parties involved will be able to understand. In a short pitch, one of the most difficult things to recover from is a listener not understanding what you do, and 90 seconds leaves little time for clarification with someone who's completely lost.

3. How do you create value?

Entrepreneurs need to clearly communicate the value of their idea or solution and who will benefit from said value. If you fail to mention how you are creating value, you will have trouble convincing your audience that you, the inexperienced student, can solve the problem you presented. To help avoid this problem, it is important you quickly show you are knowledgeable of the market and your competition. Focus on how your solution is better than that of your competitors, not on why the competitors' solution is worse, and be very careful when name-dropping competitors as you don't have time to go into detail.

4. Why you?

This is probably my favorite question to ask as it always yields a wide variety of answers. Can you answer the "why you" question? If we were practicing your pitch together, I'd ask you this question over and over and over again because it typically takes a fair amount of struggle, thought, reflection, and awkwardness before the best answer emerges. What is the best answer, you ask? It's the answer that best helps you sell yourself and/or your team. When giving a pitch, you need to convince your audience you are highly capable of executing on the solution you are presenting. This confidence needs to be expressed through your tone and body language, which typically requires hours of practice with a variety of audiences.

How to Answer the Four Questions

There are an infinite number of ways to deliver an excellent pitch. The most successful pitches, however, are those that answer the four questions uniquely and authentically using storytelling.

1. Uniqueness: Entrepreneurs always try to incorporate their own unique flair into a pitch, whether through language or props. Creativity is always encouraged but can be risky, so be sure to do your due diligence and know your audience. I recently saw one student entrepreneur rap his 90-second pitch. It worked for his particular business and audience, but it wouldn't have worked for many others.

2. Storytelling: Using a story-based structure to communicate your problem and solution will help you connect more strongly with your listeners and ensure that your audience recalls your pitch more clearly after the fact. Information travels best when disguised in a story, so make the story a Trojan horse for the content you want the individual you are pitching to remember.

3. Authenticity: Judges and investors know how to bring out the real you whenever you are pitching, and they do so because they want to see how invested and connected you are to your company. An inauthentic entrepreneur is a big turnoff for investors. You need to remove the "sales person" from your pitch, relax a little, connect with your audience, and clearly communicate that the problem-solving solution you've proposed means a lot to you. Show listeners that your company is something you truly believe in.

The Art of Practice

It is very important that you practice your pitch in front of a wide array of audiences, as first impressions of your pitch from people of different backgrounds will likely be the most valuable feedback you receive. Once you collect enough feedback, you'll see patterns emerge that will guide you toward the ways in which you should adjust your pitch. As a rule of thumb, practicing your pitch at least 20 times in front of no fewer than 10 different people should be the bare minimum.

Also, don't try to memorize your pitch verbatim, as you'll be thrown off completely if you forget even word word. Plus, your pitch should be customized to your given audience, which means it should vary a little with each presentation. When putting together your initial draft, read it aloud to yourself four or five times. Your goal should be to make the core components of your pitch flow naturally and not sound scripted.

The Art of Listening

Pay close attention to any questions your practice audiences ask and take the time to write them all down. Once you've practiced enough, you'll begin to see patterns in the questions. These patterns are valuable in two ways: They will let you see where you are not communicating effectively, and they will show you the areas where you need to come up with a standard stellar response. Remember: Your ability to respond to questions in real-life pitches will typically determine if you get the next meeting, and in competitions the Q&A session is where the judges separate the good pitches from the winning pitches.

Sell Yourself Fast

According to *Business Insider*, it takes around seven seconds to make a first impression. And according to Microsoft, the average adult attention span is now only eight seconds. That leaves an incredibly narrow window to make a strong first impression that captures your audience's interest and ensures they decide to actually listen to the next 80 seconds of your pitch. Then, in that 80 seconds, you hope they learn enough about what you are trying to do to want to meet and ask you for more information.

Sheldon Barrett, pictured above at the 2015 Future Founders uPitch Competition awards ceremony, is a mechanical engineering student at The University of Florida. Sheldon's pitch is his story. He tells of how he needed to drink fresh coconut juice when he was ill, but due to his frail state, piercing the coconut shell was too difficult. While recovering on medical leave from school, he put his engineering skills to good use and created the Cocovana, which is essentially a corkscrew for coconuts that makes cutting a small hole in the shell so easy anyone could do it. He then patented his invention.

For his pitch, Sheldon attached magnets inside the back of his Cocovana t-shirt as well as on the backside of a laminated copy of his issued patent. At the point in his pitch when he had to answer the "Why me?" question, he "magically" produced the patent protecting his idea by placing it on the table in front of the judges. Ultimately, Sheldon's pitch was little more than his story, but it was truthful, it conveyed him as an expert engineer who developed his own solution to a problem he knew all too well, and it was memorable.

Sheldon rehearsed his pitch, repeatedly, for over a year, entering multiple competitions along the way. Here's how he made out: 2014 UF Entrepreneurship Club Pitch Competition Winner, 2014 CEO Nationals Semi-Finalist, 2015 Southeastern Entrepreneurship Conference 2nd Place Winner, 2015 GAIN FastPitch Winner, 2015 CEO Nationals Finalist, and 2015 Future Founders uPitch Competition 2nd Place Winner. Oh, and $6,000 in prize money just for rocking a 90-second pitch. To learn more about (or to order) Sheldon's product visit www.cocovana.com.

"Our 368 Kickstarter backers were our brand ambassadors, our proof of concept, and our focus group. They helped launch our company."

– Roberto Torres
Serial Entrepreneur

Generating PR Buzz for Your Startup
Patrick Snyder

Few things can be more impactful for a new business than frequent, positive press coverage. The idea that public relations (PR) happens organically or that you'll get media attention based solely on having a great product is a dangerous myth – waiting for organic coverage is a direct path to not getting noticed.

Anyone who has ever taken PR 101 will tell you to write and send press releases containing the five W's: Who, What, Where, When and Why. Writing a good press release is a skill you should develop, but there are some great sites with templates to help you get started, including MediaTrust.org (mediatrust.org/get-support/community-newswire-1/tips-and-faqs/what-do-i-include-in-my-press-release) and Netpreneur.org (netpreneur.org/news/prmachine/pr/rules.html).

That said, what your PR 101 friends won't tell you (perhaps because they don't know) is that there is massive competition when it comes to getting PR, so you're going to have to beat out all of the other companies looking to grab headlines by being more compelling, resourceful, entertaining, or funny than they are. PR is a game, so make your PR strategy all about winning.

Over the years I've helped clients gain national coverage from the *Chicago Tribune*, the *Los Angeles Times*, *Forbes*, *Digiday*, ABC's *Secret Millionaire*, and CNN, as well as countless local outlets. I've reflected on my experiences, both successes and failures, and put together a list of my top four tips for gaining media exposure for your new venture.

#1: Build Your Own Press List

You can write as many spectacular press releases as you want about your company, but until you have contacts to send them to, you won't get any press. When building a press list, you should choose quality over quantity. The gold standard is to have a relationship with every editor, writer, and producer on your list. In the long run, it's much better to have 10 excellent contacts that you know will consider your releases than 1,000 that have no clue who you are. When building your list, start by identifying all the key individuals involved in covering the news relevant to your business, following them on Twitter, and genuinely engaging with them. If they post an article you like, favorite it; if they post one you think your followers would like, retweet it with a comment. People typically pay attention to those who engage with them in a positive way on social media.

Next, identify the top three to four people from the two media outlets most relevant to your business and ask for a meeting. (You can always Skype with them if they're not local.) Playing the student card will increase the odds they'll take you up on your offer, so don't be afraid to do that. At the meeting, ask if it's OK for you to send them press releases on newsworthy topics, and if so, find out if they typically want photos/videos included and what submission format they prefer (e.g., email, thumb drive, fax, etc.). Let them know that, as a student, you're looking to get fluent in the press process so you can make their lives easier and that you appreciate the time they're taking to help you learn. And as always, remember to follow up afterward with a short thank you note.

Once you've established a basic relationship, it's time to cultivate it further. PR is a lot like sales in that members of the media tend to do business with folks they like, so stay in touch with your contacts and be a good resource for them by offering to help however you can. Send them a nice note when you see an article from their publication. Become memorable, show you care, and they'll be more likely to listen.

#2: Shop Local

Many entrepreneurs discount the value of local press, especially when their venture targets a national market. This is a flawed strategy, as local press coverage can create a ton of secondary value. When you get your release picked up locally and "on the wire," your odds of being covered at the national level increase dramatically. Countless of my national media hits have been due to initial coverage in the local press.

Let's compare some numbers. My experience has been that when a local outlet runs my story, it creates the equivalent of about $600 in ad value, which is significant to most startups. Furthermore, when a local story is picked up by national outlets like the *Huffington Post*, the ad value estimate jumps closer to $60,000, which is of great value even to bigger businesses.

#3: You Must Benefit the Reader

The job of any editor or producer is to create the most interesting content possible for their audience given what is available to them. No matter how great your media list may be and how much editors, writers, and producers love you, they will not run a single word you have written unless it benefits their readers in some way. Remember, your releases are nothing more than a pitch to the press, so they must be compelling, resourceful, entertaining, or funny. While editors and producers are hungry for content, the content must still be worthwhile for both their publication and their audience alike.

Let me show you what I mean. Below is an example of two different press releases on the same topic: a national hotel chain offering a special for couples on Valentine's Day.

1. This press release announces fabulous new lovers retreat packages and some very special menu items to please every romantic. Gourmet cuisine, rooms with a view, and other surprises, including a prize package of a trip for two to Hawaii, await those who book now.

2. This press release announces a contest for the "Perfect Kiss" video with winners to be announced on Valentine's Day. The lucky winners will receive a prize package containing a romantic weeklong trip for two to Hawaii. "Perfect Kiss" videos can be submitted online on the company's website where the public will then vote for the winner.

Of the two releases, which do you think will garner more media attention? While they both contain much of the same information, option two is much more likely to get noticed. The premise behind the "Perfect Kiss" contest is much more entertaining than the packages that are the focus of the first press release, and the gamified online voting element in the second release gives readers a way to engage as a spectator or participant.

#4: Events Are a Great PR Tool

Hosting or sponsoring events can be an easy way to get media exposure since events are typically considered newsworthy by default. Part of my charge as the executive director of USASBE is to promote the organization and our supporters, and event-based PR has been very fruitful for us in this regard.

In 2014, I created the Public Forum on Entrepreneurship Excellence. We worked with our local university partner to line up a great venue and interesting speakers, but we still needed to a hook for the press. To overcome this hurdle, I reached out to the office of Wisconsin Governor Scott Walker and asked him to consider proclaiming May 5th as Small Business and Entrepreneurship Education Day across the state. I knew Governor Walker was interested in promoting business and education, and I also knew his press staff would be working hard to further his agenda. Not surprisingly, Governor Walker agreed to make the official proclamation and speak at the event, which came with a bonus of having the use of his full-time press corps.

Thanks to Governor Walker's involvement with the Forum, we ended up being mentioned in over a dozen publications, including an article in *U.S. News & World Report* that ran in 15 different languages. The total advertising value for the event's press coverage totaled over $60,000, which was a massive return considering the fact that the event cost us nothing.

#4: Sending Out a Press Release Is the First, Not Last, Step

Doing nothing more than sending out a blanket press release is a pretty passive approach to getting media coverage. Once the release is written, there's still a lot of brand selling to be done, and I can tell you with absolute certainty that the more you proactively promote your brand to the press, the better your results will be. In a past life, I worked with billionaire businessman and best-selling author Steve Kaplan. Despite being an incredibly successful businessman, Steve was not well known, which made promoting him to the press difficult. Our solution was to have him take any speaking opportunity he could get, even if unpaid, as a means of getting his name out there more.

Before each of Steve's speaking engagements, we would send a press release. At that point, the work was just beginning. For example, on the day before Steve's talk to the Atlanta Area Chamber of Commerce, I sent all the Atlanta-area editors and producers this website of Steve's media clips to help promote Steve's brand: http://www.stevekaplanlive.com/wp-content/themes/entrepeneur/action.php. Then, on the morning of the speech, I dropped off donuts at the local newsrooms as a means of getting my foot in the door to remind the press of Steve's talk and the newsworthiness of it all. Doing so let me find out if the reporters had any special needs or would like to have a one-on-one interview with him before or after his talk. Often these extra touches would not only get us added coverage for Steve's live event, but also land us in the online versions of the newspapers by noon that day.

We would leverage any Chamber of Commerce or Rotary Club speaking gig we could get as an opportunity to build Steve's brand and sell more of his books. Ultimately, we ended up building a nice public speaking business for him as well, booking corporate events for companies like Panasonic, AT&T, Frito Lay, and Oracle at as much as $30,000 per hour. It took time and multiple failures to learn how to pitch reporters well. Sometimes we would walk away $20 poorer having given away doughnuts, and other times we'd get huge wins worth $20,000 or more in ad value. The key is to treat the PR process like a sales pitch: expect rejection, have a plan for overcoming it, and keep on pitching with a smile on your face.

I serve on the USASBE Board of Directors and have witnessed Patrick's media prowess firsthand. When putting together content for this book, I knew I wanted to include an entry on gaining media exposure, but I also knew I had to go about it carefully. Too often entrepreneurs fall into the trap of wanting to get maximum media exposure as quickly as they can. This is a misguided strategy, as you typically don't want exposure until you have tested your value proposition and proven your market fit. Once this is done and your production is scalable, have at it, but until these conditions are met pump the breaks and invest your time 150% toward ensuring you are creating real value. Furthermore, entrepreneurship is currently a trendy topic in many local markets, so student-backed ventures can usually pick up attention easily. If this happens to you, you'll likely see an uptick in your web traffic, and you'll also gain some legitimacy points. For most businesses this is a blessing, but remember that it's not very sustainable in the long run – you must have other, stronger means by which you market your company.

"It is every man's obligation to put back into the world at least the equivalent of what he takes out of it."

– Albert Einstein

Launching a Nonprofit Startup

Ramon Aleman

In the process of launching my nonprofit startup, Unhoused Humanity, I've learned a number of things that I'd like to share with you. During the past year, I watched 63 people get off the streets and find homes. I saw $5 turn into $35,000. I've felt complete joy, and I've also felt bitterly overwhelmed. Most importantly, however, I've seen something that started out very small turn into something great, which is the biggest motivation I could possibly give you, my fellow students, to follow in my footsteps and work toward making the positive change in the world we all so desperately need.

Just Start

People spend years promising that one day they'll get started – just not today. The right time is always "after I finish this" or "after I finish that." The human mind is great at creating excuses out of fear. Like Lao Tzu once said, "The journey of a thousand miles begins with one step." Although it seems so simple, taking the first step is truly the most difficult part of any process.

So how exactly should you start? Take your grand vision for what you'd like to do and break it down to its smallest component. For example, if you'd like to create a nonprofit that provides mentorship to at-risk youth, start off by finding and mentoring a single teenager. If you do a good enough job, that one teenager will eventually refer another. Now you have two.

It really is as ridiculously simple as it sounds: If you are truly creating value with your work, you'll see a snowball effect once you get started. When I launched Unhoused Humanity, I wanted to house everyone in America, but I chose to start with raising $1,000 for a single person using a GoFundMe campaign. Once I hit my goal, momentum got going, and in the 12 months since we have been able to house 63 people. Start small and start now.

Be Transparent

Over the past year, I've learned that total transparency is the most important characteristic of a nonprofit. Donors want to know where their money is going, so show them. It is difficult for huge nonprofits like the Red Cross or United Way to keep overhead low and show their value on a case-by-case basis, so as a smaller, more agile organization, you have the upper hand.

Watsi and New Story Charity are two tech nonprofits that went through Y Combinator, the top startup accelerator in the world. Watsi crowdfunds for healthcare, and New Story Charity crowdfunds to build homes in Haiti. Both organizations have been incredibly successful due to the fact that they provide their donors with a photo update of the exact patients or families they helped to support. In addition, both charities separate their finances into two accounts, one for administrative costs and one for providing aid. By doing things this way, it is very easy to prove that all funds raised are used to help beneficiaries, which helps supporters feel as if they are making maximum impact with their giving. I've tested out this method found it to be hugely successful, so I highly recommend you follow a similar model as well.

The Ask

To work in the nonprofit world, you must be comfortable asking: asking for advice, asking for connections, and most importantly, asking for money. The first step to making a successful ask is to identify what it is you need and who is the most likely to give it to you. Always do your research on the individual you'll be asking; use tools like LinkedIn to identify their interests, passions, and connections and use that information to your advantage.

The next step is the hardest one: Make the ask. When I first started fundraising, I was afraid to ask for money. When the time came, I would circle around the question and ultimately leave the meeting with a new relationship but no actual donations. With the help of a mentor, I learned that there is no reason to fear the ask; after all, being told "no" is the worst thing that can happen. After I faced my fear of rejection, donations skyrocketed.

Last but certainly not least, the third step is the follow-up. Donors by nature are typically very busy people, and thus it's not unusual for them to unintentionally forget their commitments. To avoid this setback, set yourself a reminder to follow up with your donors via phone or email to confirm everything is on track and ensure they make the donation they initially promised.

Go Above and Beyond to Say Thank You

When you're first getting started, you don't have the benefit of a lengthy track record to lend credibility to your organization. Thus, your first supporters – the people that believe in you despite a lack of supporting evidence – are taking a risk by trusting in you. Reward their risk by going above and beyond to genuinely thank them and make them feel special, whether with a note or with another form of recognition (e.g., a plaque). Not only will this open up a world of opportunities and connections, but it will also give you a competitive advantage over bigger nonprofits who are too large and unwieldy to follow up with personal thank you notes. For example, whenever a donor gives a gift through our website, we send them a personal thank you video from our team and tell them exactly how much their donation means to us. This makes people feel great about donating to us, so much so that they often make repeat gifts and refer their friends to us.

Avoid Burnout

Launching a student startup is a difficult process that takes a ton of time. It's extremely easy to get off track, become overwhelmed, and burnout. One semester, I made the mistake of letting my nonprofit consume my entire life, and I started sacrificing personal self-care for organizational progress and growth. There was no time for exercise, and no time for healthy eating. In fact, even while I was relaxing, Unhoused Humanity was on my mind.

It is very easy to trick yourself into believing you must always being doing something to maintain growth. This is a myth; do not believe it. Instead, detach yourself from your organizational outcomes and remember your value as a human being would not shrink if everything failed tomorrow. Motivation is very important to success, but ultimately, you are not your startup.

Pictured above is Ramon with 71-year-old Jimmy, the first person Unhoused Humanity was able to get into a home. Jimmy became homeless in 2003 when his wife died, which caused his emotional and financial life to come crashing down around him. He spent 12 years without a home before Ramon and Unhoused Humanity came in and helped him fill the void between what he earned and what he needed to find and retain housing. Ramon said it perfectly above: start small and start now. All too often we fail to take any action, yet as Ramon has demonstrated, consistent small steps can result in huge impact (and traction can snowball). What action step will you take today to get your business or idea moving forward?

"Without publicity there can be no public support."

– Benjamin Disraeli
Former British Prime Minister

Revving Your Startup's Promotional Engine

Betsy A. Hays

If you think before you act, you will always win. But what should you think about? To get your startup's promotional engine revving, I suggest you spend some time thinking about my most favorite framework for just about anything: the five W's and the H.

What

What are you trying to accomplish with your promotional strategy? The most obvious catch-all goal is building awareness of your business and its products/services, but that's not enough to pay the bills. What do you need to do to make the sale? Do you wish to build your reputation? Do you want to generate referrals? Be 100% clear on what you need to get out of your PR efforts before moving forward to avoid wasting time and effort.

Who

Who do you need to talk to in order to accomplish your what? The worst promotional strategies are directed at "the community" or "the public." Those groups are very, very, very rarely who you should actually be targeting. Sure, if your product is for sale to the public, technically every member of the public is a potential customer. But is that really the case? No! You need to identify the specific groups of people (or businesses if you are B2B) that are the most likely to do what you need to be successful. The more homogeneous these groups, the easier your life will be, as you will need fewer individual messages and media channels to reach and resonate with everyone. The broader your target, the harder you make your life.

Think about it this way: Who are the "low-hanging fruit" that are most likely to purchase from you? These folks should be your biggest priority along with the people who influence them. Sometimes you can have better luck reaching influencers and having them speak on your behalf than going after customers directly. To identify the influencers you'll need to sway, ask yourself who your target audiences are most likely to listen to and/or where they go when they need advice.

After you identify your target audience, get to know as much as you possibly can about them. Things like age, marital and family status, education level, motivations, and lifestyle habits will provide valuable insight when it comes to putting together appealing messaging. Don't know where to start? Ask a librarian. There's a great deal of valuable research out there, and most librarians are fountains of knowledge who are more than happy to help those people who take the time to stop by and ask them in person. (Side note: Always default to talking to people in person. It's the best way to get anything done. Hiding behind your phone or laptop is counterproductive.)

Where

Where does your target audience go for information? Are they active on social media, and if so, which platforms? Are they big TV watchers or newspaper readers? Do they prefer to get their news offline or online? What shows do they watch and what magazines do they read? What sites do they visit most online?

This is not *Field of Dreams*. You don't want to build it and hope they come. Instead, you need to make sure to be where they already are. Find out where your audience gets information, and then go there and give them your information! Don't expect them to seek you out, because it's not going to happen. You're the one that's got to do the legwork.

When

I'm sure you're familiar with the phrase "timing is everything." Well, it's an adage for a reason. Timing is key to effective communication. Discover the times of day and days of the week when your audience is most tuned in and communicate with them during those times. For social media, there are a number of great (and free!) analytics tools that can help you find out the best times/days to post, and some platforms like Facebook even have analytics built right in. Check out websites like Tweriod and Twtrland – they can help you find your most influential followers and track which Tweets are getting the most engagement. If you need more information than you can find, go straight to the source and ask your audience directly. And if you can't ask, conduct A/B tests to assess what works and what doesn't.

Why

Why should your audience care about you and what you have to offer? WIIFM ("What's in it for me?") is the strategic communicator's favorite acronym. The "me," of course, refers to your audience in this case. What benefit is it to them to do what you want them to do? Articulate clearly and frequently why it is in their best interest to engage with you. Clarity is key, as when things are unclear people tend to tune out or move on (and you don't want that to happen to you). To avoid this pitfall, test your messages on people outside of your industry. If they don't understand what you're saying, your audience won't either.

As a student entrepreneur with a new startup, you have some PR advantages right off the bat. To begin with, "new" is always more interesting than "not new," so that's the first thing you've got going for you. Furthermore, if you can somehow add "cool" to your "new," then you increase your chances of generating word-of-mouth buzz significantly, which is one of the best (and cheapest!) ways to increase the visibility of your company.

How

Once you've answered all of the "W" questions, it's time to move on to the "H" and figure out how you will get your message to your target audience.

First, get your branding ducks in a row. Create a logo and slogan that make sense based on all of the above thinking (who you are targeting, what you need to say to that target, etc.). Also, do some research and experimentation before making design choices so you can ensure that the color palettes, fonts, etc. you select are representative of the image you want your company to portray. And finally but perhaps most importantly, once you settle on a style, make sure to use it consistently throughout everything you create.

Next, you've already gathered some information on where your audience typically gets information, so you'll want to start there. Study up on the rules of engagement for your audience's favorite channels so you can communicate as effectively as possible. Some tips to get you started:

- Social media – Create, find, and share content that will help you position your company as the resource for information on your industry/space. And don't forget that shorter is better when it comes to encouraging others to share your content.

- Traditional media (news) – Pitch stories that are newsworthy. Watch or read the outlet you want to pitch so you know what reporters typically cover (and how), and match your ideas to their needs.
- Websites – Use fewer words and more visuals. Tell your story in small pieces across multiple pages to entice visitors deeper into the site. Don't give it all away at once.
- Posters, fliers, postcards – Keep it simple and don't forget your call-to-action and contact information.

Looking at the bigger picture, here are some helpful keys to success:

- Be honest, even when the truth isn't pretty. If your customers don't trust you, they won't buy anything. Tempted to weave a tale instead of telling the ugly truth? Do a little research into companies who cover things up and get exposed. You'll change your mind quickly.
- Tell stories. The best communicators are the best storytellers. What are the stories that make your business special and interesting? Do you have any special anecdotes about your employees, customers, or partners you can share?
- Be authentic. Be who you are and share the real version of you and your business. The public can smell fake from a mile away.
- Ask directly for what you want, even if it is obvious. No one is a mind reader. Don't assume anyone, including your target audience, knows what you want from them. Tell them explicitly what you'd like them to do.

Form Partnerships

More than likely, you will never have enough money, time, or resources to do everything you want to do. That said, by being smart and forging strategic partnerships from the outset, you can tap into others' resources and create mini economies of scale that help make easy work of what would have been impossible for you to achieve on your own.

Generally, nonprofit organizations make great partners. When you're looking to form a relationship, select the nonprofit whose mission most closely mimics and/or complements your own. For example, if you are a financial services business, you might want to partner with a non-profit that promotes financial literacy. If your space is children's toys, you might look for an organization that helps foster children.

Recently my students were putting on a Multimedia Production Day to recruit students to major in multimedia production, and they partnered up with the local Community Media Access Collaborative (cmac.tv). As part of the deal, CMAC streamed the students' event live and also provided free memberships to the winners of the competition the students held as part of the day's festivities. The event helped CMAC gain visibility, and the partnership helped my students borrow a little credibility from CMAC's established reputation and put together a better, more far-reaching event in the process.

And Then What?

Once you've been actively implementing your PR strategy for a while, be sure to check-in and evaluate. Entrepreneurs don't have time to do things that aren't valuable to their business, so let's make sure you are spending your PR time wisely.

My favorite easy-to-implement evaluation structure is start-stop-continue. Think about what you need to start doing, what you need to stop doing, and what you need to continue doing. Write these things down, prioritize them, schedule them, and you will be well on your way.

> The notion of finding a strategic PR partner and borrowing credibility is a good approach for many startups, and if you combine it with the "host an event" suggestion Patrick Snyder mentioned, you can really begin to see how you could build some serious traction. Personally, I've been trying to use start-stop-continue ever since Betsy's first draft of this chapter was submitted. It's not as easy or as simple as it sounds, but if you actively reflect on your activities from the past week, you can begin to recognize what changes you need to make. For me, start-stop-continue has made me rethink saying no. I need to learn when and how to say no and get better at actually saying it. I've got to stop doing tasks that create no value simply because I was too naïve or afraid to say, "No, I cannot continue to do X, Y, or Z. I'm sorry."

"Sometimes, idealistic people are put off the whole business of net-working as something tainted by flattery and the pursuit of selfish advantage. But virtue in obscurity is rewarded only in Heaven. To succeed in this world you have to be known to people."

– Sonia Sotomayor
U. S. Supreme Court Justice

Purposeful Networking
Beth Bridges

The most powerful thing you can do right now while you're in school is build your network. Challenge yourself to deliberately and intentionally create strong connections and keep those connections long after you graduate. If you do, you'll

- have a vast head start regardless of where you go to school,
- acquire a powerful skill that will serve you all your life,
- be able to rapidly create beneficial relationships if you relocate,
- and build your business much more quickly than those who don't network.

Networking helps you tap into other people's experiences, get introductions to suppliers and buyers you wouldn't otherwise find, and gain exceptional credibility with everyone. Networking can also help you sell more products and services. Whether you started your enterprise for the experience or the money, making a profit is the whole point. Networking will get you closer to profitability at a better ROI than anything else you can do next to having a great product or service.

Here's the mistake even experienced business people make: They try to make sales while networking, not because of networking. Networking is not the place for selling, but it can lead to more sales. When you network, you gain visibility, exposure, and access to more resources, which are natural precursors to building a strong and successful enterprise.

Overall, networking is a positive, affirming activity that will put you in regular contact with like-minded people who are encouraging and willing to lend a hand. You'll meet people who can help you grow your business by showing you how they did it, introducing you to joint venture partners, and/or getting you in with people who can be your advocate or advisor.

The Negative Side

Sometimes networking will be frustrating and annoying. If you haven't yet had the experience I'm about to describe, you will. But I want you to be prepared, to understand the context, and be ready to shake it off. You cannot let one or two time-wasting experiences turn you away from one of the most effective life and business tools you'll ever have.

Here's how it usually happens. An acquaintance calls and says they'd like to take you to lunch to show you something or to just catch up. When you show up, they launch into a full-blown presentation about the new multi-level marketing organization they've just joined. When someone did this to me, they actually went so far as to pull out a portable DVD player and set it up in the middle of the restaurant table.

(Side note: I love the part of the business model of multi-level marketing where the more someone helps the people below them be successful, the more successful they are. What I don't love is the part where they call it "network marketing" and encourage people to sell to people under the guise of networking.)

Back to the lunch. Multi-level marketers are taught to handle things in this way because the people who are teaching them know the answer to "Do you want to get together so I can sell you something?" is almost always going to be no. That's why real networking is so important to network marketers. If you build trust and give value first, the door will be open to your request.

Do you see how this works for you too? Whether or not you're in a multi-level business, people don't want to feel like they're a prospect and not a person. We all like to buy, but no one wants to be sold to.

A Valuable Graduation Gift

Building your network will build your influence as well as your confidence. You'll become a stronger communicator. You'll learn how to find out what people want and then you'll learn how to help them get it. Why? Because that's how you'll get what you want. Your ability to connect with people from outside your immediate work/life/school circle will be one of the most worthwhile things you can take away from your collegiate entrepreneurial experience. It will be the best graduation gift you give yourself.

There may be times in your entrepreneurial or employment journey where your network is going to be the most valuable business resource you'll ever have. And sometimes it may be the only resource you've got besides your brains, enthusiasm, and energy. All of which should be applied to building your network. You can do a great deal with just those things.

How to Build Your Network

Networking is simple, but like so many things, not always easy to do. I have a definition of networking which is, I admit, a little bit long, but it is the most complete explanation that I've ever found: "Networking is the ongoing process of building long-term, mutually beneficial relationships by sharing ideas, information, resources, and experience."

Your network is made of the people with whom you connect and interact. Professors, fellow students, family, friends, and business community members should all be considered part of your network.

Your current network may be so small or narrowly-focused on campus that the majority of people you're spending time with have very similar backgrounds and ambitions to yours. You can and should build relationships with your fellow students, but you'll also need connections with people who are further along in experience than you are. These usually aren't college students, so you're not going to find them by staying in a narrow corridor between work, school, and home.

You've got to expand outside your current network to expand your influence. Much of the power in a network comes through the "weak ties." These are your friends of friends. They may be familiar with completely different sets of people, companies, and organizations than you are, so they'll have opportunities for you that few or any of your peers will have heard of. This is where you'll get the most value. So how do you expand your reach and build a network?

The Simple Plan

I created this networking success plan to provide business people with a deliberate, specific, and intentional networking process to follow. It's incredibly simple but not always easy to put into practice. There are only five parts to it, and they are all understandable, straightforward actions. If you apply just one or two of these parts to your regular actions, you will be networking. Follow them in a series, over and over, and you'll begin to make a strong habit of networking that few people ever master.

1. Believe in _____: Believe in yourself and believe the process of networking, over time, will bring you the results you want.
2. Go places: Focus on places and events that are designed for networking and that bring together people who have similar interests in building connections.
3. Meet people: When you are in the right places, you can be confident the people there are interested in meeting you and looking to learn how they can help you and be helped by you.
4. Stay connected: It will take time to build relationships, so find a way to see them again at future events and connect with them on social media to build on what you learned when you met them.
5. Give value: Learn what people want and then find a way to give it to them if you can.

Each of these steps is simple. If you're already doing them, focus on doing them more consistently. While you do not need to be doing a lot, taking regular action to meet new people and then staying in touch with them along the way is a critical part of building a successful network.

The last step, giving value, is something most people find difficult to do. As a college student you might think you don't have a lot time to share with people, or money to spend on their projects or products, or experience they would find valuable. Whether that's true or not, you do have one thing nearly every businessperson will love for you to give him or her: Your sincere attention.

Zig Ziglar said it best, "You can have everything in life you want if you will just help enough other people get what they want." Give them the value of your attention and appreciation. Maintain the connection and some day, down the road, they'll return the favor.

"Have no fear of perfection – you'll never reach it."

– Salvador Dali
Spanish Surrealist Painter / Cultural Icon

Waiting For Perfect When Good Will Do

Eric Liguori

In the spring of 2014, I hired a team of undergrads to help plan a global conference to be hosted in Tampa, FL. The team included two students, Hailey Lindbergh-Lewis and Amanda Moore, and its main function was to finish an enormous to do list (process registrations, send out updates to attendees, order conference supplies and swag, design and assemble a program and name badges, etc.).

Amanda and Hailey showed up to work one afternoon to find me going back and forth on some trivial decision. I was obsessed with perfection to the point of inaction, and despite having promised them a decision that afternoon, I still didn't have one. They had provided me with ample information and a few great options, but I was unsure as we had some major sponsors involved that I didn't want to disappoint. Another 90 minutes passed before they re-entered my office a bit frustrated and proceeded ask what else I needed to know before making a decision. Still feeling flummoxed, I'm certain I responded, "I don't know."

This is the point in the conversation at which I opened the door to ambush. Earlier that day Amanda and Hailey had learned about the "70 percent solution" in their negotiations class, and now it was their turn to teach me. The rule states that "if you have 70% of the information, have done 70% of the analysis, and feel 70% confident, then move." It's a fairly simple principle based on the notion that a "less than ideal action, swiftly executed, stands a chance of success, whereas no action stands no chance. The worst decision is no decision at all." Floored, I told them to go ahead and make the decision on their own so they could move forward.

I was instantly in love with the 70 percent solution and wanted to know its origin. I flipped through the few negotiations textbooks I have in my office to no avail, so I kept digging only to find this was a Marine Corps philosophy. (For future reference, the military is a phenomenal thought leader on topics of strategy and leadership.) Intrigued, I ordered David Freedman's *Corps Business: The 30 Management Principles of the U.S. Marines* and quickly discovered the 70 percent solution is incredibly relevant to multiple aspects of entrepreneurial decision-making.

As Freedman states:

> Still, making quick decisions in the face of incomplete, uncertain, or undigested information is not easy, and it's especially discomforting when you know that a mistake could cost you your own life and the lives of your colleagues. But Marines get used to it, says [Colonel Thomas] Moore. "Everyone is always looking for perfect truth, but you never have it," he says. "Even if you did have it, the other guy is up to something, so by the time you execute it your truth isn't perfect anymore."

Certainly entrepreneurs aren't typically risking their lives and the lives of their colleagues, but very often we are risking our livelihoods and the livelihoods of our employees (not to mention any friends, family, or fools who invested in the business). It's important to exercise caution in situations such as these as well as in how you interpret the 70 percent solution. By no means does the solution condone knee-jerk decision making or fast and furious style planning; instead, it instructs you to do your research, to understand all the key factors you can, and once you have a plan with a good chance of success, to act!

I've been a huge fan of the 70 percent solution ever since Amanda and Hailey first introduced it to me. I use it myself, I tell students to use it, and I insist companies I am involved with use it. In March of 2015 some former students of mine and I were preparing to attend One Spark, the world's largest crowdfunding festival boasting 275,000 attendees, to not only crowdfund for some projects we had been working on but to also potentially pitch to investors. We were in crunch mode with only five weeks to prepare, as we found out on March 1 that we had been accepted into the festival that ran from April 6-12. One of the first things we did was grow our team by a few people to help get us where we needed to be, and then we scheduled weekly calls as a formal means of checking in. Of course more informal meetings took place in between the calls, and a plethora of emails and Facebook posts also ensued.

A few days before our first full group call, I received an email from Shervin Zoghi, founder of the International Organization for Developmental Entrepreneurship (IODE; one of 3 projects we had lined up to present at One Spark). In the email were some mocked-up graphics we needed to finalize and get to the publisher, and he noted that we can discuss further and get everyone's feedback on the upcoming conference call. I vetoed that decision, pushing that we move forward. On the next call, when the graphics were brought up, we instead discussed the 70% rule. Shervin was the lead for the project and co-founded the organization, I was on the board, and we had buy-in from Alan Suarez, IODE's other co-founder. Running this discussion past four more people was not an effective use of our very limited time; we had our 70% so it was time to move forward.

We used this rule going forward with other decisions we made, though we never discussed it again. After forcing yourself to be OK with 70 percent solutions and calibrating your mental information percentage calculator, it becomes a much more tacit process. All in all it took me about six months to really start to feel I was past doing the "mental math" of differentiating 70% from 60% or 80%. For me the hardest of the rule's three criteria is the last one (feeling 70 percent confident). I still find on occasion that even with 70 percent of the information collected and 70 percent of the analysis completed, I am at best 50/50 on confidence. I think this very scenario is why the 70 percent solution is so effective. In easier situations you can quickly hit your 70/70/70, and in more difficult ones you are forced to really gut check what you are doing. As an entrepreneur, you'll often be taking huge risks that could jeopardize your livelihood as well as the livelihoods of others, so there's nothing wrong with taking the time to ensure your plan has a good chance of working. Long story short, the 70% rule offers startups a great ROI.

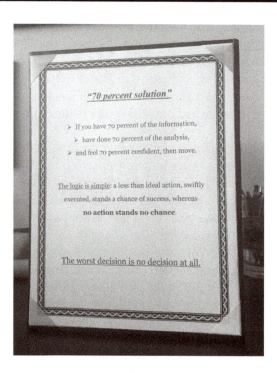

> ## "70 percent solution"
>
> - If you have 70 percent of the information,
> - have done 70 percent of the analysis,
> - and feel 70 percent confident, then move.
>
> The logic is simple: a less than ideal action, swiftly executed, stands a chance of success, whereas **no action stands no chance**.
>
> The worst decision is no decision at all.

Amanda and Hailey later made me a 70 percent solution certificate that now sits framed on a bookshelf in my office as a constant reminder. More recently, as this book was in the copyediting stages, I stumbled on some related words of wisdom from Louis C.K., America's King of Comedy, that I think you'll enjoy. C.K. stated to GQ's Andrew Corsello his 70% rule for decision-making:

These situations where I can't make a choice because I'm too busy trying to envision the perfect one—that false perfectionism traps you in this painful ambivalence: If I do this, then that other thing I could have done becomes attractive. But if I go and choose the other one, the same thing happens again... So my rule is that if you have someone or something that gets 70 percent approval, you just do it. 'Cause here's what happens. The fact that other options go away immediately brings your choice to 80 because the pain of deciding is over. And when you get to 80 percent, you work. You apply your knowledge, and that gets you to 85 percent! And the thing itself, especially if it's a human being, will always reveal itself—100 percent of the time!—to be more than you thought. And that will get you to 90 percent. After that, you're stuck at 90, but who the fuck do you think you are, a god? You got to 90 percent? It's incredible!

"My viewpoint is ONE data point. I might be wrong. Get lots of data points. Mix mine into your pot and see how it settles. I'm not always right, but I'd rather tell you what concerns me than to sweep it under the rug."

– Mark Suster
General Partner at Upfront Ventures

Tips for Being a Successful Entrepreneur
Mike Pronovost

My story as an entrepreneur began in high school. Like many others, I questioned which career path I should take. I looked around at all of the students older than me in college and wondered why we study so many years of our life only to graduate and get put into a minimum wage job. I knew I had great talents and skills I could share with society, but in my mind, they couldn't be put to use without being in an executive-level position. This was discouraging to me because I didn't want to wait to be in my fifties before I could showcase what I could do for our society. I was impatient, and I wanted to start making a difference now while still being a high school student.

My light bulb moment happened when I saw a copy of Forbes magazine with Mark Zuckerberg on the cover. Zuckerberg, in case you've been living under a rock, was changing the world with a little company called Facebook despite being only 23 years old at the time. I thought to myself, "This guy figured out how to make a difference without having to sink years of his life into the corporate ladder. How can I do that?"

As I read more, I learned about something called "entrepreneurship" and how it is one of the only career paths that allows society's brightest to shine no matter their age, background, or standing in life. And even better, I discovered that entrepreneurs don't need a special degree or even any specific qualifications. The idea of entrepreneurship – that I didn't have to spend years waiting my turn to contribute to society – gave me a whole new outlook on life because it opened a door for me to share my talents without being told I was too young or inexperienced. I truly believed people would benefit from the products or services I could offer, so I did what every other 16-year-old high school student would do: I got a seller's permit and became a CEO.

The Learning Curve

To put it very bluntly, being a 16-year-old CEO was scary. I read tons of business books and surrounded myself with as much information as possible, but no amount of education could have prepared me for what I had taken on. The learning curve was massive. (I don't say that to scare you. I say that so you'll embrace it and move forward anyway.) There were many times I questioned whether I should keep going. I had friends with part-time weekend jobs who were guaranteed to come home with a paycheck, whereas I was spending countless hours working on my business without knowing if I'd make any money at all.

As scared as I was at the time, I wouldn't trade my experience for anything. The most important thing to remember when starting your first business is this: It's not about making money. Yes, I said that correctly. You will rarely, if ever, succeed your first time. You wouldn't expect to ride a bike perfectly the first time, would you? But please, don't get discouraged. The failure isn't really a failure at all; it's the education phase of entrepreneurship. You're learning what you should and shouldn't do through trial and error, and you're learning how to organize yourself, your schedule, your business plan, and your customers.

Be Prepared to Fail and to Learn from It

So how did I do the first time? The answer is not well. I did manage to piece together a small amount of business, but it wasn't nearly enough to keep me going. I failed, but I learned an important lesson in the process: You have to have a great marketing or communication plan. I didn't understand the relevance of marketing a product to a specific group of people, so I foolishly and wastefully advertised to the masses to no avail.

I decided to take a second crack at things a few years later when I turned 18. This new company was called Powerband, and it brought high speed Internet to rural users who only had dial-up. Ironically, I actually wasn't trying to start a business; I only wanted to solve a problem. But upon realizing how happy people were to get my solution, I knew that I needed to make it into something more. And something more it was indeed, so much so that it paved the way for everything I've done thus far.

The key takeaway here is that I wouldn't have been successful on my second try if I hadn't failed on my first. Over 90% of startups fail, but many of those failures convert to successes the second or third time around. Each new venture is a fresh start, and it only takes one to succeed. If you prepare to fail and learn from your mistakes, you'll be stronger and more likely to win in the next round.

Don't Be Afraid to Share Your Ideas

Although I found success with Powerband, I still had my share of slipups. Now that I had something good going, I was convinced I shouldn't share my business ideas with others because they could potentially steal them. So I held my ideas close and kept to myself. In hindsight, I realize my paranoia was ill-founded. Most entrepreneurs don't need or want to steal ideas. Why? They've got hundreds of their own, and they don't have the time or motivation to start an entire company off of a fleeting idea they overheard. Furthermore, I regret depriving myself of all of the feedback I could've received had I been willing to let others in on my thoughts. The feedback could've given me a new perspective that would've allowed me to improve and make things even better than they already were.

It Takes Time

Success doesn't happen instantaneously. Steve Jobs is quoted as saying, "Pixar is seen by a lot of folks as an overnight success, but if you really look closely, most overnight successes take a long time." Don't feel discouraged by small growth, and prioritize quality over everything else. It's more important to deliver a great product than a mediocre product with larger sales. Likewise, if you only have one customer, focus on that one customer as if he or she is your ticket to growth. And as you grow (and you eventually will if you focus on quality), continue to treat every customer like they're the only one, even if they're not anymore.

As a Student, You Hold More Power Than a Large Company

Lastly, I want to share a story that my mentor once shared with me. I never understood it when I was younger, but I do today. I highly recommend you keep this in mind as you start your business. My mentor told me, "I'd rather own a very small business or startup where I'm the only employee than a large company with thousands of employees." I always wondered why he would say that given that he's a business mogul who owns a $300 million company with over 1,000 employees. You would think it would be easier being larger because you have a vast number of resources, a larger customer base, economies of scale, etc.

The real truth, and I only realized this recently, is that I too would prefer to be a one-man show instead of a large enterprise. When you're the only employee, you know you will be the one to handle every customer. You have more control over the quality of your product and the way your customers are treated. The minute you expand, you lose part of that control. Your profitability grows, sure, but the risk that the quality of your offering or your customer service will become diluted grows as well. All you can do is hope that your customers get the experience that you would give to each of them personally.

When it's just you, you've got to remember that you hold a huge advantage over a large company: You can make sure everything is exactly as it should be. Don't feel discouraged about being a small business or a student with limited resources. All big companies were once small businesses. And they may have even once been student entrepreneurs wondering whether they should start a business. If that's you, my advice is this: Get started so one day you too can look back and think it was the best decision you ever made.

It seems the two Mikes are at odds. Earlier Luchies said no one man alone can build an empire, and here Pronovost notes he prefers being a one-man show. You have to decide what works best for you. What's consistent with your style, your preferences, your experience, and your vision of the future? Empires are not built solo, but empires are also not for everyone.

"Software innovation, like almost every other kind of innovation, requires the ability to collaborate and share ideas with other people, and to sit down and talk with customers and get their feedback and understand their needs."

– Bill Gates
Co-Founder, Microsoft

Launching New Products

Eric Liguori & Prashant Joshi

For the better part of the last seven years, Prashant Joshi has spent his time running special projects and launching new products almost every day. He began his career in 2008 in the Technology Commercialization Program (TCP) in the Lyles Center for Innovation and Entrepreneurship, and by 2010 he was promoted to TCP director. During this time he also worked as a consultant in the California Small Business Development Center network and taught upper-division college courses in opportunity assessment & feasibility analysis. In 2012 he accepted a position at Lakos Corporation running special projects and launching new product lines, and shortly thereafter in 2013, Lindsay Corporation (http://www.lindsay.com/; NYSE Symbol: LNN) acquired Lakos and did a reported $690.8 million in revenue. Today he serves as Lakos' Business Development Manager focusing on sales and marketing for both domestic and international markets.

From his unique career trajectory, Prashant has developed extensive experience in product development and launch as well as an in-depth understanding of the knowledge and skills entrepreneurship students need both inside and outside of the classroom. Knowing this, I asked Prashant to deliver a guest lecture to the Executive MBA students enrolled in my spring 2014 graduate entrepreneurship seminar. After hearing his remarks, which included invaluable advice for aspiring student entrepreneurs, I followed up with him in 2015 to interview him for this book. Below is a summary of our discussion, with my questions in bold.

Tell me about some of the products you've helped take to market?

I'll start with my time at TCP and then talk about the corporate perspective at Lakos. While at TCP, I was partially involved in launching Click (an espresso protein drink available for purchase on Amazon.com), Pilloroo (a themed pillow product with an internal storage pouch and stuffed animal), Poparazzi (a vintage bottle cap jewelry business), and TurnAid (a device to turn elderly people in bed to prevent bedsores). Some launches were successful and some were not, but regardless of the outcome, I always found the process of taking on a new product to be incredibly exciting and interesting. For example, I loved going through the process of familiarizing myself with a new industry and competitive set before each launch. It takes a tremendous amount of time and effort, but it is a fascinating process that is absolutely critical to success. Too many times I've seen otherwise successful companies fail simply because they misunderstood the competitive factors at play within their industry.

Launching new products is one of my primary job functions at Lakos. Since starting in 2012, I've launched five new water filtration and purification products, all of which led the industry with unmatched efficiency and performance and large distribution networks already in place. That said, launches are prone to hiccups, even with a superior product and established distribution. I've learned to avoid pitfalls by devoting time and effort to staying on top of customers' needs and preferences. Understanding pain points and being able to articulate how your product helps alleviate customers' problems is a critical part of the product development and launch process for any business, whether a startup or Fortune 500.

In your experience, where do the best ideas come from?

Idea generation ultimately leads to execution and potential success. What often goes unrealized, however, is the huge number of ideas required to achieve a single launch. Students often fail to start with a large enough pool of ideas, partly because they don't spend enough time brainstorming and partly because they latch onto the first good idea they have and don't explore other (perhaps better) options.

When developing and launching a new product, what's the one piece of advice you would give student entrepreneurs?

Fail fast. To explain what I mean, I'll refer to a conversations I had with one of my mentors, Mike Sommers. Let's say ideas are like eggs. Mike said he believed entrepreneurs should start by throwing all 12 eggs at the wall and seeing if a chicken comes out. I argued that something was missing from Mike's process, as finding a chicken doesn't guarantee anything, and Mike agreed. So we added another step: Once you find a chicken, you should immediately throw it out of a window to see if it can fly.

This may sound like a bird-brained example to you, and you're probably right. But the principle still stands. Complete your idea generation first before moving on to feasibility. I realize things need to happen quickly and that you shouldn't waste too much time before moving on to execution. But that being said, if you don't start with a large enough pool of ideas (potential pain point solutions) to begin with, you're reducing your chances of executing on something that will be able to fly on its own.

How do students and corporations approach product development differently?

In my experience, corporations diversify their efforts and simultaneously work on a variety of different ideas in various stages of development. Students don't hedge their bets in the same way, thus increasing their odds of failure. Once a student finds a flying chicken of an idea, they make that one idea their sole mission until it either succeeds or fails.

Speed is key in new product development. You have to move fast. Everyone would like to have more data or to keep modifying the product until it's "perfect," but that's not a recipe for success. Companies who excel in product development move new products out fast and tweak after the fact if needed. Let your customers begin using the product and tell you what you should change; don't waste time trying to figure it all out for yourself. As a student or small startup you have mobility to your advantage, so don't forfeit that strength and fall into the trap of analysis paralysis.

You raise some interesting points. As you answered the last two questions, I thought back to the notion of an idea funnel. They say that for every great idea, 10,000 people conceived it, 1,000 people figured out how it might be done, 100 people generated specific solutions, 10 people made the design actually work, and only 1 made the invention stick in our culture.

Those numbers are not surprising. Large corporations spend a lot of time generating hundreds of ideas that are eventually whittled down to dozens through research and experimentation, then to tens, and then to the top three for launch. Startups are at a disadvantage if they don't begin with multiple ideas and iterate their way down to the best one. If you start out with tunnel vision, how can you expect to compete against a giant, resource-plentiful corporation with an unblended perspective?

Is there anything else relating to new product development you think students need to know?

Yes. I often tell new employees there are five factors for entrepreneurial success within any organization, and I think these factors are just as applicable to a student startup. The five factors are as follows:

1. Right Team – Having the right team is critical for new product development. The ideal team member is a doer with a diverse skillset who is fully committed and capable of learning additional skills as needed. A small team is typically best, so I advise applying the one pizza rule (i.e., the entire team must be able to be fed off of only one pizza). I guess you could interpret that rule to mean that you should pick skinny teammates, but really it implies that you should find the right two or three smart, dedicated people and then focus on action, not management.

2. Clear Focus – Like I just said, you have to focus on action. I'm sure you're familiar with the business model canvas, which has a box titled "Key Activities." For a startup it's best to think of this box as a prioritized to-do list. What are the three, four, or five most critical tasks on your list? Do you spend 90% of your time working toward crossing those off of the list? If not, you need to reevaluate how you're spending your time.

3. Defined Timeline – If you're like me, you get much more focused on the tasks at hand as the deadline begins to loom closer. Having a set timeline is a great way to generate motivation as well as measure progress and predict future growth. It will help you know if you're moving forward, how quickly you're doing so, and what barriers are preventing you from moving as fast as you could be.

4. Executive Support –This may not seem relevant for a startup, but it is. In a large organization you need management support to secure and allocate resources, among other things. You need support as a startup as well, but just from different parties. Do your family, friends, and significant others support your vision, and can they help you in a meaningful way? What about your investors – what level of support do they provide, and what do they expect in return? Support from multiple constituencies is a critical part of the process.

5. Be Realistic – Entrepreneurs are known to be unjustifiably optimistic, so this is especially important for startups. Stretch goals are great, but being realistic with yourself and those around you is the most important thing you can do. Make plans based on conservative projections grounded in real data from real customers. Do you truly believe, and can you demonstrate with data, that you have a good product?

"As a restaurateur, my job is to basically control the chaos and the drama. There's always going to be chaos in the restaurant business."

– Rocco DiSpirito
Celebrity Chef, Author, Restaurateur

So You Want to Open a Restaurant...

Dean A. Koutroumanis

American entrepreneurs have long had a standing love affair with restaurants, so much so that the restaurant industry employs more people in most states than any other industry (with the exception of state government, of course). Why is this? Could it be the freedom of individual interpretation inherent in the culinary arts? Is it the love of serving and interacting with people or the desire to become financially secure? Or perhaps the ego boost that accompanies owning a restaurant? The answer is all of the above and then some.

Many immigrant families who came to the United States in the first half of the twentieth century eventually ended up owning and operating their own restaurants. As a result, Americans were inundated with a cultural and culinary diversity that has since become mainstream. Just look at pizza, America's favorite food. In 1905, Lombardi's Pizzeria opened in Little Italy, New York, and it still operates in the same location today. Family-owned Columbia Restaurant in Tampa, FL, now on its fourth generation of management, also opened in 1905. Similarly, my family's own Yorkside Pizza and Restaurant in New Haven, CT has been serving the Yale University community since 1969 and was recently named one of *USA Today*'s most iconic college restaurants.

The secret formula behind these longitudinal success stories – hard work, long hours, perseverance, conceptual renewal, understanding, family support, and more hard work – reveals the difficult truth that lies beneath the glamorous surface of the industry. It's no secret that most new restaurants fail, and the majority (60%) do so within the first year of business. The industry is also notorious for employee turnover, with estimates ranging from 100% to over 400% depending on what segment of the industry you're in. Furthermore, startup costs are very high, often running well over $100 per square foot, yet asset liquidation prices often net only 10-15 cents on the dollar. And to make matters even worse, owners typically work seven days a week to the tune of 80+ hours total.

Given this outlook, why in the world would anyone want to open a restaurant? Entrepreneurial spirit, that's why. Today's aspiring restauranteurs are driven by the same passion and desire to build a long-lasting concept that motivated the founders of Outback Steakhouse, Hooters, Papa John's, and many more. And it was these same desires that drove my partners and me to form our first restaurant corporation in 1993 and begin working on a concept. After two years, in May of 1995, our dream became a reality when we opened our flagship restaurant, Antonio's Pasta Grille.

During my nearly 25 years in the business, I've had a hand in developing five different concepts in eight locations. Most of these ventures were successful, but my partners and I absolutely had our share of failures as well. Through it all, I've learned a number of important lessons that I'll share with you now. My students fondly refer to them as "Dr. K's Five Top Tips for Aspiring Restauranteurs."

#1 Uniqueness of Concept Design

Think outside of the box and do what no one else is doing. When putting together your concept, you should aim to differentiate yourself by developing an innovative, creative, and unique core competency that can serve as your competitive advantage. Five Guys Burgers and Fries' core competency of fresh, never frozen, hand-pattied beef burgers and fresh-cut fries was different enough to allow them to build a massively successful company in a saturated market. Todd Graves, founder of Raising Cane's, did the same thing with fresh, never frozen, chicken fingers, and Cane's now has over 225 locations spanning 19 states.

When my partners and I opened our flagship Italian restaurant, we wanted to create value for our customers. Our competitive advantage was multi-serving portions at single-serving prices – one full pound of pasta, to be exact. When we set plates down on the table, our customers' eyes would often bulge out of their heads. Nobody ever finished the full pound, but they always took doggie bags to go and would later return for more. In fact, our restaurants won "Best Pasta" in Tampa Bay for 18 consecutive years. As an independent restaurant, we didn't have big advertising budgets, so we used our core competency to help build our business.

#2 The Power of People

People play the biggest role in any restaurant, far above and beyond the food. And by people, I mean customers and employees. Customers drive our business – they are the reason we continue to exist – but employees ensure we are successful with our customers. Restaurant jobs are notorious for being tiring and difficult, and turnover is higher than that of any other industry. Why is this? I blame it on poor leadership, poor management, and a lack of quality organizational culture. It is critical to develop an organizational culture in your restaurant that encourages cohesiveness, teamwork, loyalty, and a sense of family, as these values will help you develop and retain happy employees who feel a sense of commitment toward you and your business. Empower your employees to do their job, and don't micro-manage them. You'll be surprised at how well they perform.

In our restaurants, we were fortunate to have many employees with extremely long tenures, which we attribute to our culture. In fact, we had one employee who was with us for more than twenty years who would drive 45 minutes each way to work. She passed more than 500 other restaurants on her commute, yet she worked for us. If that is not commitment, I don't know what is.

#3 Be the "Mayor"

You are one of your restaurant's biggest competitive advantages. Thankfully I learned this lesson early on in my career. When we opened our first restaurant, we were obsessed with quality, so we spent most of our time in the kitchen expediting food and watching every detail. One day, a long-time, successful restauranteur who was one of my mentors pulled me aside and asked me why I wasn't in the dining room. According to him, overseeing the food wasn't the most important aspect of the business – building relationships with customers was. I ended up taking his advice and hiring a supervisor to watch over the kitchen so I could focus my time and energy on our patrons.

Research has shown that figurehead and/or spokesperson is the most important role an independent business owner can play. It is critical that you greet everyone who comes into your restaurant. Shake hands, kiss babies, and visit tables. Get to know your customers and make them regulars. Everyone wants to return to the place where they are made to feel special.

#4 Change and Adapt

The old adage "nothing is a guarantee" is a lie. In business, there is one guarantee: change. Every business and every product has a lifecycle, and some lifecycles last longer than others. As Charles Darwin eloquently stated, "It's not the strongest of the species that survives nor the most intelligent, but the one most responsive to change."

There are many forces at play in our businesses, some we can control and some we cannot. Let's look at social media, a socio-cultural force that has a profound impact on the restaurant industry. Yelp, Google, Facebook, and many other social media applications have given a voice to restaurateurs and customers alike, and the impact has been both positive and negative. Whether you like social media or not, it is a force to be reckoned with, and ignoring it won't make it go away. People change, times change, and tastes change; to survive, you must stay on the cutting edge of innovation as it pertains to your business.

#5 How much money do I need?

A lack of planning is the second most common reason that startups fail; a lack of capital is the first. The restaurant business is very deceptive when it comes to cash flow. Unlike many businesses, you will generate cash flow from the first day you open your doors. This early influx of cash give many new restauranteurs a false sense of security, so much so that they end up spending every available dollar on capital assets with the assumption that money will be available as soon as they open for business. Unfortunately, bills often have a way of growing faster than the money does, leaving you unable to cover all your costs.

We fell into this trap when we opened our first restaurant. We struggled to keep up with the bills, and to add insult to injury, we had opened in the dead heat of the Floridian summer (the slowest time of year). My partners and I went 4 ½ months without taking one penny of salary, and when we did eventually pay ourselves, it wasn't much. Having seen restauranteurs make this mistake over and over and over again, I've developed a solution: Calculate the total cost of everything you need to open your restaurant and multiply it by two. That's how much you'll need. There will always be cost overruns in your startup, and there will always be things you didn't account for. If you raise the appropriate funds and have the working capital you need, you can focus on the critical factors of running your restaurant once you're open for business.

Nothing about the restaurant business is easy. That said, it can be an incredibly rewarding career for those who have the passion and commitment to persevere. There is no question there were times I questioned what I was doing, especially in the beginning, but in hindsight I wouldn't trade my experiences, relationships, successes, or failures for anything.

In August of 2015, I had the pleasure to visit Yorkside Pizza and Restaurant in New Haven, and I must admit it was clear why Yorkside was rated one of North America's "Most Iconic College Town Food Joints" by the Huffington Post and Spoon University in 2015. Thanks to the efforts of the Koutroumanis family, the restaurant has truly become an integral part of the culture that makes Yale such a special place. To this day, generations later, alumni still return to the restaurant to grab a slice of their favorite pie or enjoy the award-winning Greek salad. Dr. K's advice is well-grounded in life experience: failures, successes, and even a little dumb luck. Don't underestimate the work you need to put in, the startup capital you need, or the role of luck in making your restaurant a success. Perhaps only the first two are requisite, but the third certainly doesn't hurt to have.

"Most of the important things in the world have been accomplished by people who have kept on trying when there seemed to be no hope at all."

– Dale Carnegie
Author, *How to Win Friends and Influence People*

Learn to Sell

Eric Liguori

Sales are fuel for a startup. They provide cash flow and signal to investors you are on to something. Ergo, startups require sales to survive, and until you have actual sales validating your business model, everything is a guess. Guess, a short five-letter word, is arguably one of the most dangerous words there is to a startup. Guessing indicates the presence of both risk and uncertainty in your model. It means you're OK with violating rule #1 of the lean startup movement: building a product nobody wants.

The obvious challenge most student startups face in generating sales is a lack of resources. The vast majority of student-run businesses cannot afford to hire a dedicated and experienced sales staff, so they're left with two alternatives: Either violate rule #1 or themselves learn to sell. I highly recommend the latter option, and given that it's your time and money on the line, I'll assume you do as well.

Selling is an acquired skill. While many seasoned sales professionals will tell you selling takes years to master, you can acquire some basic sales skills pretty quickly if you put forth the effort. Unfortunately a recent study published in *Harvard Business Review* noted that fewer than 22% of accredited undergraduate business programs (and only 3% of accredited MBA programs) have formal sales coursework. And, even in the few places where formal programs exist, only a small percentage incorporate sales courses into their entrepreneurship curriculum, which means you're on your own in figuring out one of your largest success factors.

To address this deficiency, I started a sales skills boot camp for student startups in California in 2013. "SOLD! An Entrepreneurial Sales Skills Boot Camp" is a six-week long immersion into professional selling. Over the course of the program, I bring in seasoned sales professionals to work with students, employ online sales training content, and host a Q&A panel discussion and networking session with relevant professionals in the field. As of January 2016, "SOLD!" is now offered annually in Massachusetts and Florida.

Unfortunately, it's difficult to translate the hands-on, immersive nature of the "SOLD!" boot camp experience into words, or I would do that for you here. That said, I think sales skills are too critical to omit from this book completely, so I've spent some time reflecting on the last few years of "SOLD!" programs to put together a list of what I would consider the top sales lessons student entrepreneurs need to learn before launching their startup.

1. You can learn by doing, but it's not easy.

"Don't take sales as a negative; look to embrace it because it's going to test your metal. Sales is a grind; I look at it as a siege, but it's a very enjoyable siege. I'm out reinventing myself every day. It's how you present yourself and relate to your customers. You just have to go out and start selling; you won't get your basic rules of sales in school; you'll develop them in the trenches actually selling." – Joe Kelly (Senior Sales Exec. at Johanson Transportation)

2. Ethics are everything.

"My strongest piece of advice for anyone in sales is never, ever, ever promise something you can't… well, never promise anything you don't intend to try and do. There are times when you are going to commit to something and find out later it's just not going to happen. That happens. Obviously you want to minimize those, but it does happen. And don't lie. It's amazing to watch sales people who will say something that is completely, totally, blatantly made up. And you know what, it catches up to you, and when it does you have absolutely no credibility whatsoever. That's something I don't think you can ever overcome." – Matt Cholakian (Business Development Manager at Hydrite Chemical Corporation)

3. Build up to the big "Yes" by soliciting a series of smaller yeses.

Dr. Bob Levine is an expert in the art of persuasion. Levine discussed the principle of gradually escalating commitments (or, making you say yes by never saying no). "Sales people using this technique begin with small requests and then give the prospect time to reset their acceptable anchor points. Then and only then do they escalate to their next request." In his book *The Power of Persuasion: How We're Bought and Sold*, Levine adds, "The principle of slowly escalating commitments can be thought of as the grammar of effective persuasion. It's the temporal dimension…Wait until everyone has committed little by little to the doctrines of the program, let inertia settle in, and only then pop the big question."

4. Bring your "A" game.

"One of the best things we've found in sales is to take people by surprise. The reality is half the time, especially if I don't have glasses on, I look like a freaking cheerleader from Connecticut, and people expect that from me. They'll come in and say, 'Oh, are you going to bring cupcakes to the meeting?' or 'You definitely don't have the same technical knowledge as someone sitting next to you.' I think it's just an assumption, it's a stereotype, and one of the ways around that is to be on your 'A' game so that you can surprise people and instantly become more memorable." – Tracy Edwards (Client Services Executive at Subdirect)

5. It takes time; be patient and persevere onward.

"It's a slow, manual process, especially at the start." That comes from one of my personal favorite "SOLD!" case examples of Y Combinator mentors who routinely preach about how manual a process it is to gain an initial user base. Airbnb Co-Founders Brian Chesky and Joe Gebbia flew to New York every week to meet with early Airbnb hosts, coach them on pricing strategies, offer photo taking tips, ask for introductions to other potential hosts, and then personally pitch those new prospects.

Wrapping it up.

Time, practice, and failure are requisite parts of your journey toward becoming a salesperson. Developing finely tuned sales skills is tough to do solely in an educational environment, and as we've already discussed, most universities don't even offer opportunities for doing so. And to make things even more complicated, selling on behalf of a startup is a harder-than-usual type of sales due to a lack of brand recognition or a track record of success. As Matt Cholakian noted above, you have to derive your credibility as a salesperson from yourself, not your organization.

Please know that I'm not trying to paint a grim picture, nor am I trying to make this sound impossible. Sales is a numbers game, but what isn't? Michael Jordan missed more shots than he made, Margaret Mitchell's *Gone with the Wind* faced rejection 38 times before being published, and Pandora.com's founders approached investors 300 times before securing funding. Selling is hard, but thankfully there are some great resources available to help you along the way.

Sales4Startups (www.sales4startups.org)

Sales4Startups is an international organization that teaches sales skills to technology startups, but even non-tech startups can learn from this collective of seasoned pros. They regularly host events and workshops, and they also send out tips via their blog and email lists. Action step: Join their mailing list.

Jeffrey Gitomer's Work

Jeffrey Gitomer is the author of two fantastic books on sales: *The Sales Bible* and *Little Red Book of Selling: 12.5 Principles of Sales Greatness*. Both books were sought-after door prizes during "SOLD!" and highly recommended by the "SOLD!" speakers. I've long said "entrepreneurship requires action," so my favorite take away from Gitomer is B.T.N.A. or "big talk, no action," a phrase for those times when you're "too busy bragging about the sales you are going to make and not busy enough making them." Action step: Hit up the library and read the books.

Startups Heart Customers (www.startupsheartcustomers.com)

Startups Heart Customers is a fantastic website created by Greg Skloot, former president of the Northeastern University Entrepreneurs Club, co-founder of VC-backed Attend.com, and current VP of growth at Netpulse. It's packed with great content, offers loads of links to additional resources, and dishes out some candid sales reality. Action item: Check out the site and be sure you watch Alex Baldwin's speech on closing the sale from *Glengarry Glen Ross*.

"You shouldn't focus on why you can't do something, which is what most people do. You should focus on why perhaps you can, and be one of the exceptions."

– Steve Case
Co-Founder, AOL

The Deal With Accelerators
Greg Horn

Joining an accelerator program was a lifesaver for my most recent startup. My co-founders and I all had other full-time obligations when we launched, so our schedules were stretched quite thin to say the least. Luckily for us, we won a competition that gave us some early funding and office space on the campus of Lehigh University in Pennsylvania. For our first year, we operated out of that office while splitting time with our jobs and studies, even though we all not-so-secretly wished we could devote ourselves fully to the company and move to the Bay Area to pursue the Silicon Valley dream.

When we finally did quit our day jobs and move out west, it was a huge leap of faith for all of us. We had virtually no funding and only a handful of revenue-generating clients. What we did have, however, was confidence that we could make it work. Even before we moved, we were already applying to Bay Area accelerator programs with the help of AngelList. A few months after arriving in our new home, we made the final round for the Boost accelerator program run by Adam Draper, whose father and grandfather are both legendary venture capitalists in Silicon Valley. The fact that we'd already made the move definitely helped our chances, as it allowed us to attend interviews in person and also demonstrated that we were serious about committing to the company on a full-time basis. Eventually Boost accepted us, and we began a three-month live-and-work program based out of San Mateo, CA in November 2013.

Before deciding whether or not we would join Boost, my partners and I had some decisions to make. Boost offered us $15,000 in cash, a place to live, shared office space, access to a great mentor pool, and lots of other perks in exchange for 6% equity in our company. Giving up the equity was a tough pill to swallow for us initially, but after a conversation with one of our mentors, we changed our view. Drawing upon a passage from The Founder's Dilemmas, he told us that we should take the Boost opportunity for the potentially huge upside – after all, 6% of a company as fledgling as ours was at the time was worth next to nothing.

Unfortunately, even with the accelerator's help, we ended up not getting any funding for our venture. That said, our accelerator journey was definitely a positive one. We developed strong friendships with the other accelerator participant companies' founders, learned a ton, and worked with some amazing mentors. Below I've listed some of the common questions I get about our accelerator adventure as well as my answers to them. My hope is you'll be able to benefit from our experience and be more familiar with what to expect should you ever have the opportunity to join an accelerator yourself.

Is an accelerator right for me/us? If so, what kind of accelerator?

Because there are so many different types of accelerators out there today, there is likely a program that is right for you and your company. A few things to consider:

1. Solo Founder - If you're a solo founder and want to keep it that way, an accelerator may not be right for you. Most accelerators ultimately want you to scale, which means they'll likely pressure you to bring on partners before too long.

2. Lifestyle Businesses - There are plenty of entrepreneurs that simply want a business that generates enough revenue to live the life they desire, and there is absolutely nothing wrong with such an approach. As I mentioned above, however, most accelerators are looking for you to scale, so if that's not in your plans, they probably won't be interested.

When it comes to the type of accelerator you should join, I recommend keeping your mind open to many different possibilities. Some accelerators only focus on certain types of markets or companies, but there are also plenty that are open to everyone. We took the approach of applying to any and all that were relevant to our industry and tailored our application to each accelerator's specific goals. As with anything, you want to put yourself in their shoes and tell them what they want to hear which, in this case, is how your company will help them achieve their goals.

Am I ready for an accelerator?

If you're not willing to move and there are no accelerators in your area, then no, you may not be ready. Most programs will want you to relocate to be near them for the duration of the program, but thankfully many of them will also help you find housing.

Also, like most investors, accelerators typically will want you to be a C Corp so they can be added to your Cap (Capitalization) Table. If you're not a C Corp currently, most programs will be willing to wait for you to make the switch – but know that you probably won't get a check from them until your status is officially changed.

What are accelerators looking for in the companies they invest in?

Every accelerator has its own unique goals, but they are all ultimately looking for companies that have the potential to scale up to the point of having an exit, whether via acquisition or going public. Long story short, they want to make sure they're going to make money off of their investment in your company.

What can I do to give us the best chance of getting into an accelerator?

To increase our chances, we focused on tailoring our pitch to the specific goals or niche of each accelerator. We also made sure we had our message tight. It sounds cliché, but you really do need to have your elevator pitch perfected. If you can't clearly communicate what your company does in three sentences or less, then you've got some work to do.

On top of the above points, you want to have a strong "why." For help with this last point, look up Simon Sinek's fantastic TED talk, "Start with Why." Sinek talks about how great companies achieve greatness by having a strong purpose for what they do. If you have a compelling "why," it'll be much easier for someone to get behind what you're doing.

Lastly, find a few strong mentors that will look good on your applications. Not only will this increase your chances of getting selected, but it'll also help you run your company better! I highly encourage all entrepreneurs to have at least one or two mentors at all times.

Are the terms favorable to us? How do I know I'm not giving away too much?

I don't know what terms are good for your company, but I do know that you should find a mentor who can. In our case, the 6% equity share was hard to give away, but our mentor made it clear that without an accelerator's help the 6% wasn't worth anything at all in the first place. Once we were given that perspective on things, our decision was a no-brainer.

If your company is growing so fast and furiously that you think you don't need any extra help, then maybe you don't need the help of the accelerator. Or maybe you feel that the given accelerator's group of mentors isn't that strong and won't be helpful to you. Think about it like this: Many people say the biggest reason to go to Harvard or Stanford is their student and alumni network. Graduating from those schools gives you instant credibility and instant access to influential people you otherwise may have never known. The same goes for accelerators – if you get into Y Combinator or 500 Startups, you've got instant credibility. And if the accelerator has access to some fantastic mentors in your field, that alone could be worth the price of admission.

How can I differentiate a good accelerator from a bad accelerator?

This is definitely difficult to do, but a few things come to mind:

1. How long have they been operating? It is helpful to understand how much experience they have in working through the tedium of helping startups succeed.

2. How many batches of companies have they gone through? This might be even more important than knowing how long they've been operating. The number of batches they've been through (and how many companies were in each batch) will give you an indication of what they've seen and done. This is not to say that a brand new accelerator should absolutely be avoided, but depth of experience is at the least a good place to start your evaluation.

3. Have they had any exits? Most accelerators will not have had any exits unless they've been operating for at least three years, so don't be discouraged if they say no. If they say yes, however, that's a huge plus. Try to determine exactly how the accelerator

contributed to the exits to better understand what you stand to gain by working with them.

4. Who are their mentors? Mentors are one of the biggest benefits to working with an accelerator. While it's important that the folks running the accelerator are great mentors, you also want to be sure there are other mentors on tap who can help you with what you'll need.

5. What does the program do to facilitate work with the mentors? This was something we learned on the fly. Boost did "mentor speed dating" in which we spent 20 or so minutes with each of their mentors to figure out who was the best fit for us and vice-versa. After the speed dating sessions, it was totally up to us to work with our mentors as much or as little as we saw fit. Other accelerators may do things differently, however, so it's a good idea to understand the extent to which the program will facilitate work with mentors.

6. Talk to companies that have been through the program. This is huge. We requested to chat with a few companies that were in earlier batches at Boost, and the information we gained played a big role in our decision to join. Our conversations with them also help us fast-forward and visualize where we could end up after the program. If you decide to go this route, I recommend requesting to speak with companies similar to yours, as that will provide you with the best possible point of comparison for use in your decision-making.

What is the best way to apply to accelerators?

As I mentioned earlier, many accelerators have applications on AngelList, which allows you to save a ton of time and effort by repurposing a single profile for multiple applications. In addition, having your ducks in a row in terms of describing your company, your trajectory, your plans for funding, your near-term goals, and other similar topics will make it easier to apply. Other than that, it's a matter of putting yourself in their shoes and positioning your company to fit what you think they want.

I first met Greg and his co-founders in a bar in Chicago about two months before their startup, Gigawatt, entered the Boost accelerator. Near the end of Gigawatt's time in Boost, I invited him to campus to speak about the experience. The day before Greg's visit, the Gigawatt team completed their final "official" dry run demo to prepare for the upcoming Demo Day. When Greg arrived, I remember being struck by the pairing of excitement and nervousness he and his team were experiencing. They knew they were at the make or break point where they'd have to either raise some capital or pull the plug. Pictured is Team Gigawatt (Jake, Roger, Jacob, and Greg, from left to right) when they were first launching in August 2013.

"The more that you read, the more things you will know. The more that you learn, the more places you'll go."

– Dr. Seuss

What Successful Entrepreneurs Think You Should Read
Eric Liguori

Yes, I know what you're thinking, and you're wrong. This isn't just another list of the top 10 books for entrepreneurs, as I assume you already know you should have well-highlighted copies of *The Art of the Start, Lean Startup, Business Model Generation*, etc. on your bookshelf. Those are all b-school staples. What you'll find here is a list of lesser-known yet hugely valuable books that top-notch entrepreneurs think you should add to your cart the next time you're surfing Amazon.com.

Moneyball (and no, the movie doesn't count)

Mark Shuster, president of Orange County-based Shuster Financial Group, took over a small financial services business from his father and built it into one of the premier providers on the West Coast. Mark spoke to the students in my Executive MBA class last year, and he brought up the subject of *Moneyball* about three-quarters of the way through his talk about life, having the guts to make the ask, and what it takes to build a great business. To quote Mark, *Moneyball* is "the greatest non-business business book ever written...a must read." In fact, Mark felt so passionately about this book that he sent 40 copies to my class about a week after his visit.

Blue Ocean Strategy

Sylvesta Hall was a student in my EMBA course during the aforementioned visit from Mark Shuster. Sylvesta is a serial entrepreneur who serves as the president and managing member of Coast to Coast Petroleum and Blue Ocean Development America. As soon as Mark finished speaking, Sylvesta ran out to his car to grab a printed prospectus of his latest venture proposal, and the prospectus just so happened to highlight a business opportunity that Sylvesta deployed after reading *Blue Ocean Strategy* by W. Chan Kim and Renée Mauborgne. The premise of the book is simple yet counterintuitive: Rather than competing in crowded environments, companies can succeed by creating their own "blue oceans" of uncontested market space. While Sylvesta's opportunity was not in Mark's wheelhouse, Sylvesta did eventually secure funding and partnerships to continue development of the project, and his Blue Ocean dream continues to realize meaningful revenue growth each year.

What to Ask the Person in the Mirror

Maura Laudone, owner of Rhode Island-based Laudone Financial, was on her way to a conference in Dana Point, California when she stumbled upon an airport copy of *What to Ask the Person in the Mirror* by Robert Kaplan. In the book Kaplan talks about the importance of taking a step back to reflect and really hone in on the key factors that are critical of your organization's success. The book does get at metrics in its own way, but that's not why Maura consistently re-reads it nor why she recently purchased six copies for fellow entrepreneurs. In her own words, "I re-read *What to Ask the Person in the Mirror* often to remind myself of what am I trying to accomplish and reflect on if I am leading the way I should be leading. A career, or startup, is a marathon, not a sprint. I read it to remind me of that very basic premise."

The Boys in the Boat

Prashant Joshi, business development manager at Lakos and mentor to dozens of startups over the last 10 years, says *The Boys in the Boat: Nine Americans and Their Epic Quest for Gold at the 1936 Berlin Olympics* is an "absolute must read" for all aspiring student entrepreneurs. It's a story of how passion, hard work, and perseverance can help you go from nothing to something under even the least optimal of conditions. As Prashant notes, "You will learn through example how teamwork plays a critical role in achieving the unachievable; it's the ultimate example of overcoming adversity. I've read it three times myself, and I apply the lessons learned to every new product I launch."

Traction

Chad Spaman, president of San Marcos-based Coastal Sign & Wayfinding Inc., recommends *Traction* by Gino Wickman. *Traction* provides clear plans, tools, and strategies to get a business moving in the right direction. As one Goodreads.com reviewer put it, *Traction* lays out a six-step approach "to successfully bring a small-to-medium sized business to the next level." Chad notes that his company is currently adopting the *Traction* approach because the book "lays out the best processes and measurables [he has] ever seen."

Contagious

In addition to the great suggestions above, I'd like to personally recommend a book I think you'll find invaluable: *Contagious* by Jonah Berger. In what may be the best practical application of scholarly marketing research I've ever seen, Berger breaks down virality (a.k.a. why things catch on) into six easy to understand "STEPPS." More specifically, Berger argues that social currency, triggers, emotion, public availability, practical value, and stories are the key to rapid market penetration, and that you can proactively build the "STEPPS" into your marketing efforts as well as your core business models from day one. I've used Berger's work in class several times now, and it's always been well-received. In fact, one marketing major in my fall 2014 Introduction to Entrepreneurship course approached me after class, asked to borrow the book, and came in the next week asking to present to the class why they all needed to get copies themselves. Berger's talk at Google, available on YouTube, is a great recap of the book if you want to knock out the core content in a quick 40 minutes.

"Nearly a hundred years ago, the artist and philosopher John Ruskin suggested that the purpose of education for any person could be reduced to three questions. First, do they know where they are? Second, do they know where they are going? Third, assuming they know their desired destination, do they know what they need to know to make the journey possible?"

– Colin Jones
Author, *31 Emerging Laws of Entrepreneurship Education*

The Venture Road Map
Nelson Sebra

Starting a new venture is a journey that unfortunately doesn't always end well. All too often someone sees a business with some degree of success and is convinced he can do it too. He'll ask family and friends about his idea only to be placated with a pat on the back. No one challenges the idea itself or his ability to execute it, even though it's clear he likely doesn't have the necessary skills or experience. While his ambition and confidence is commendable, he cannot succeed on those things alone. And to make matters worse, he'll further reduce his odds of success by jumping into his new venture without developing a plan. While there is no silver bullet that can ensure success, careful planning and preparation do typically dramatically increase the odds of survival.

Let's take a little literary license and use a "road map" analogy to compare the journeys of an adventure and a new venture. Imagine someone is watching a golf tournament at Pebble Beach on television. Impressed by the beauty of the course and coastline, she decides to go see it in person. Her vehicle is in good repair, she has some cash and a credit card in her pocket, and she knows the California coast is due west from her home in Arizona. "That's enough information for now," she thinks, and she sets off on her journey. What she fails to realize is that her car has a low tire and no spare, her phone's GPS doesn't work, her credit card is maxed out, and there are no open hotel rooms within 100 miles of the golf course.

Experienced travelers would have approached the above trip differently. They would plan a route in advance, including the places they'd like to stop, they terrain they'd need to drive, and the amount of gas it would take to get there, among other things. Furthermore, they'd make advance reservations at hotels along the way and create a reasonable budget for food. They'd also likely take their cars in for a tune up before departing to make sure they wouldn't be hit with any unexpected car repair fees while on the road. All in all, they'd prepare adequately in advance to increase their likelihood of reaching their destination unscathed.

In some ways, a new venture is like planning a trip. Before getting started, it's best to use a road map of sorts to identify a clear path from idea conception to exit strategy. Below is a list my students use to chart their paths. It is intended to be a general reference that is applicable to any sort of business, although not every category may fit your particular situation.

To use the outline, first make sure you understand each topic listed and then describe in detail how it relates to your business (if at all) and how you will execute on it. I'll leave you with one simple rule to reference as you plan your journey: Overestimate anticipated expenses and underestimate anticipated revenues. Enjoy your trip!

The Chronological Life Cycle of a Business: A Roadmap

1. Idea
- How and when did you first conceive of this idea? Is it a new product? Is there really an opportunity for you to proceed with this idea?

2. Idea Feasibility
- Market Analysis
  - If you plan to offer an existing product or service, is there room for you to compete?
  - Is the market dominated by large players or spread among many smaller players?
  - Target Market
    - > Who is your potential customer?
    - > Where do they live?
    - > What are their habits, their likes and dislikes, etc.?
    - > How much do you know about them?
    - > Are you guessing who they are or do you really know?
- Industry Analysis
  - In what direction is this industry trending?
  - What opportunities really exist?
  - How soon and for how long?
- Product
  - Intellectual property
    - > Do preliminary searches on the USPTO website and/or Google Patent.
    - > Do you understand "offensive" rights?
    - > Is it really worth spending resources to register your IP?
  - Development
    - > What experience do you have in product development?

> Do you have others with experience to help you?
> Do you have access to a 3-D printer for prototyping?
> Are you working with a product development engineer?
> Are you capable of converting a prototype into a marketable product?
- Sourcing
  > Will the major suppliers deal with you?
  > Do others already possess distribution rights in your area?
  > How will you develop leverage or consideration from suppliers?
- Market Test
  - Customer Surveys
    > How will you develop questions to avoid bias?
    > How many questions will you include in your survey?
    > How many respondents will you get, and how many do you need to have valid results?
    > What is your plan for interpreting the results?
  - Focus Group(s) and Interviews
    > How many people should you include in your focus group(s)?
    > How will you decide who to include and where will you find them?
    > Who will lead the focus group(s)?
    > How will you analyze the data you collect to determine the results?

3. Business Plan
- Business Model
  - What is your business model?
  - Are you familiar with the Business Model Canvas?
  - What is your value proposition?
- Mission Statement
  - Does your mission statement accurately reflect the core principles of your business?
  - Would a stranger reading it understand what makes your company tick?
- Competition
  - Competitive Advantage
    > Who are your competitors?
    > What market share do they have?

> What is their competitive advantage?

> What are their weaknesses and how can you exploit them?

- Competitor Analysis

> How much do you know about your competition?

> How long have they been around, what service do they provide, and what niche do they serve, if any?

> Are they profitable? (Don't confuse revenue generation with profitability.)

> How efficiently do they operate?

- Form of Ownership
  - Management Team and Roles of Owners/Partners

    > Does your form of ownership provide the best opportunity to minimize taxes and attract investors?

    > Does it reduce liability?

    > Are the responsibilities of partners, investors, etc. clearly defined?

    > Does your team have all of the skillsets you need?

  - Personal Skills Assessment

    > Are you an inventor? If so, are you also a seasoned business operator?

    > Do you have the skills necessary to carry your business through the early stages of development and into the stages of growth and expansion?

- Economies of One Unit
  - Have you calculated the EOU for your product or service to determine if there are sufficient margins available using this business model?

- Pro Forma and Other Financial Documents
  - Have you prepared all the necessary financial documentation for your proposed new venture?
  - Did you use the simple rule provided in the preface – overestimate expense, underestimate revenues?
  - Cash Flow Analysis

    > Are you extending any terms to your customers?

    > Do you have sufficient capital reserves to pay your payroll and bills while waiting for your accounts receivable to come in?

    > Do you have a backup plan for cash flow shortages?

- Breakeven Analysis
  - Have you calculated a breakeven point based on known

margins and considering all factors adversely affecting the bottom line?

- Business Name
  - Does your name identify you in a positive and memorable way?
  - Is your name available as a URL for your website?
- Marketing Plan
  - Are you working with a marketing firm?
  - Have you developed you own plan? If so, what is it?
  - What is your backup plan, and have you budgeted enough to fully execute it?
- Contingency Plan
  - Nothing ever goes exactly as planned. If you overestimated on expenses and underestimated on expenses this becomes less critical. If you have been overly optimistic you may find yourself in trouble. What is your plan to stay afloat when your original plan is behind your projected timeline?
- Executive Summary
  - Can you clearly articulate your business? If you struggle telling your story it will be even more difficult to execute your plan.
- Go or No Go?
  - Remove your emotional attachment to your idea and your belief that you are invincible when deciding to progress with launching your business. If the numbers are positive and you have the right team to execute you have a better chance than most at success. Don't let your ego get in the way of making the right decision.

4. Create Entity

- Licenses
  - To open and operate any business of any type you will be required to obtain the proper licenses, permits, etc. for your specific business and pay the appropriate fees and taxes.
  - Federal
    - > Are you operating as a sole proprietorship, partnership, S-Corp or LLC?
    - > Do you have an EIN?
  - County
    - > Do you need to file a Fictitious Business Name Statement (dba)?

> Are there any other county requirements?
- City
  > Have you obtained a business license?
  > Do you need a permit for tenant improvement to a facility? Do you need a wastewater discharge permit?
  > What other city requirements do you have?
- State
  > Do you need a state-issued seller's permit and will you need to collect sales taxes?
  > Do you need to register with the Secretary of State's Office or the Franchise Tax Board?
- Bank Account
  - Based on your form of ownership do you know which documents you will need to take with you to a bank to open a business bank account?

5. Funding
- The Three F's
  - Are you using your own funds or will you involve friends or family?
  - Have you completed written documents with any of these investors to avoid future confusion or problems?
- Loan
  - Do you have sufficient collateral to qualify you for a bank loan?
  - Are you risking your home on your venture? Have you really thought this through?
- Savings
  - Are you using your savings to fund your new venture?
  - If things do not go as planned what is your backup if your savings have already been used?
- SBA
  - Are you familiar with the SBA programs?
  - Can you qualify for a 7a loan? Do you understand their rate structure?
  - Considering buying a building? Are you familiar with 504 loans?
- Grants
  - A large number of grants are usually only available to nonprofits. Have you researched to see if you qualify for any other possible grants that may be available?

- Angel
  - Are you familiar with how angel investors typically invest?
  - Are there any angel groups in your area? Do you know how to gain access to them?
- VC's
  - Do you know how to research which firms invest in specific industries?
  - Are you prepared to present a proper package to attract their interests?
  - Can you improve your opportunity with a quality pitch? Do you have resources to help prepare your documents and pitch?

6. Insurance

- Determine which are applicable of the following types of insurance are applicable to your specific business and the recommended amount of coverage and associated estimated annual cost of each.
  - Worker's Comp
  - General Liability
    - > Stand-Alone GL Policy
    - > Business Owner's Package
  - Product Liability
  - Key Employee Insurance
  - Directors and Officers Liability
    - > Errors and Omissions
    - > Malpractice
  - Business Interruption
  - Commercial Vehicle
  - Inland Marine
  - Property
  - Life
    - > Survivor Buyout
    - > Company as Beneficiary
  - Other Insurance

7. Location

- Select Real Estate Agent
  - How will you select a real estate agent?
  - Do you understand the conflict between seller's (lessor's) agent and buyer's (lessee's) agent?

- What are the typical fees and who pays them?
- Site Selection
  - Utilities – gas, water, sewage, garbage, electricity
    - > Estimate the cost of these utilities and be sure to include CAMs if you are in a center.
    - > Are you in a free standing building? What agencies do you deal with? What electrical amperage will you need? Is it already there or will it be another tenant improvement item and at what costs?
    - > Is your lease Triple Net?
    - > What other expenses do you have?
- Zoning
  - Is the space you desire already zoned correctly for your business?
  - What is the correct designation of zoning required for your business?
  - Where would you go to check the zoning of a location?
  - How difficult would it be to get the zoning changed and what is the process?
- Site Renovation and Floor Plan
  - ADA (Americans with Disabilities Act)
    - > Your business is affected by the ADA. What are the basic requirements of the ADA? For parking? For counter tops? For aisle space and shelving displays? For restrooms?
    - > What other ADA requirements may affect your business?
  - OSHA
    - > In what way is your business affected by OSHA? Inspections? Fees? Other requirements?
  - Construction Contract
    - > Assuming the location you have selected needs some modifications to properly service your need, what are the considerations in entering a contract for the improvements?
    - > If you are planning to build a new building what are the considerations? Payments?
    - > Any specific terms or conditions you would add to protect yourself?
  - Phone, alarm and music systems
    - > What type of phone system would you have installed? How many lines? Estimated cost of an installed system

and the monthly cost thereafter?
> Same for an alarm system and monitoring?
> How will you provide music for your shoppers, if applicable?
- POS System / Credit Card Processing
> Describe the POS system you will be using, its cost, and its benefits to your business
> Explain the credit card processing system you will be using, the approximate fees for each type of card you will accept, etc.
- Signage
  - What is the allowable signage per your city's sign ordinance?
  - What will that size sign(s) cost you?
  - What other requirements or limitations does your city allow or require regarding temporary signs?
- Leasing & Negotiation
  - Identify the key points you will negotiate to get into your lease and identify the items of less significance to you in terms of the lease
  - Will you negotiate the lease yourself or will someone else assist in this process? If the latter, who will it be?

8. Marketing
- Logo
  - Describe the significance of the logo, how you plan to get it created, how you will use it, etc.
  - Any need to protect it? If not, why not?
- Product
  - What products and/or services will you offer and for what market segments considering the competition? What are the alternatives?
  - The physical aspects of your product – making something with the right features to attract people who want to buy
  - What does the consumer want?
  - How and where will the consumer use it?
  - What is the branding strategy?
  - How will it be unique against competitive products?
- Price
  - What will be the range of perceived value to the consumer?
  - How sensitive is the consumer to price?
  - How is the pricing strategy comparable with competition and

substitutes?
- Does the price increase perceived value/quality of the product?
- Packaging
  - How will your product be packaged?
  - What distinct advantages does that give you?
  - Is it cost effective?
- Distribution
  - What are your distribution channels?
  - How will your product/service be delivered?
  - Growing importance of marketing channels
  - Supply chain management
  - Trends in marketing channels
  - Marketing channels and sustainable competitive advantage
- Promotion
  - What are your promotion channels?
  - What is your advertising strategy?
  - How will you increase brand awareness?
  - How do you promote differently from competitors and substitutes?
  - How will you handle promotion at the point of sales?
- Website
  - Domain Name and Web Hosting
    - > Is your domain name available? What is it?
    - > What web hosting service will you use and why and at what cost?
    - > Who will build your website?
    - > Will you personally be able to make updates and changes on the site?
    - > Are you familiar with free website templates such as WordPress, etc.? Will they work for your venture or will you need a more sophisticated site?
- Social Media
  - What role will social media play in your marketing plan
  - Who will manage your social media program?
- Advertising
  - Adwords
    - > What are the "key words" for your venture?
    - > How will you use them effectively in creating your name, your website and marketing materials?
  - Radio

> What role can radio play in advancing your business?
> What role can radio play in advancing yourbusiness?
> Does your type of business typically advertise on radio or would it be ineffective? Which channel is your demographic?
> Approximate costs to use the media?
- Print – ads, business cards, brochures
  > What type of print media can assist in advancing your business?
  > Which types will you use and in what way will you use them?
  > What are the estimated costs of each type?
- Billboard Ads
  > Is this a form of advertising that could benefit you?
  > What is the approximate cost per month?
- Trade Shows
  - Will trade shows benefit your business?
  - Identify which trade shows you would consider attending and where they're held.
  - Approximate cost of a booth at one of these trade shows?
  - What percentage of attendees are in your customer base?
- Craigslist
  - Is Craigslist a service that could benefit your business?
  - What is the cost?
  - What are the basic posting restrictions/requirements?
  - How effective is it? Compared to what?

9. Accounting
- System
  - What will be your accounting system? A simple Excel spreadsheet? Software?
  - What software should your consider or would you recommend?
  - What are the advantages / disadvantages of different software systems?
- Taxes
  - What taxes and fees are due to which agencies – e.g., state and federal payroll, worker's comp, sales tax, property tax, corporate tax (if applicable), etc.?
  - When are the taxes due? Other taxes?
- Record Keeping

- Describe the types of records you will need to keep for your business and the methods you will use in doing so.
- How long will you have to keep copies of receipts, etc. for tax purposes?

10. Human Relations

- Job Description
  - What are some of the key considerations for you when creating a job description?
  - How detailed should it be in describing tasks, duties, etc?
  - What should be included in the job description?
  - Are you fully compliant with state laws in developing and posting your job descriptions and job openings?
- Posting Job Announcements
  - Where should you post your job announcements?
  - How will you attract the best candidates?
- Interviewing
  - What are the dos and don'ts of interviewing?
  - What methodologies should you use?
  - How do you ensure compliance with state and federal laws?
- Payroll & Taxes
  - What are the payroll taxes that are the employee's responsibility?
  - What are the payroll taxes that are the responsibility of the employer?
  - What other taxes are applicable?
- PEO
  - When should you consider using a PEO?
  - What are the estimated costs of using a PEO?
  - What are the benefits?
- Retention Program
  - What is your retention plan?
  - How will it compare with that of your competitors?
  - Where does retention fit into your priorities?
- Policy Handbook
  - Describe the contents of your policy handbook.
- Family Leave Policy
  - What is the allowable time off from work allowed under this act?
  - How often?
  - At what pay rate?

- Other factors or provisions of the act?
- State and Federal Mandatory Postings
  - Obtain a list of the state and federal mandatory postings.
  - Do you understand the importance of compliance?

11. Customer Service
- Policies
  - What are your customer service policies?
  - How are they implemented and reflected in the way you do business?
  - Rewards System
- Do you have any systems you will implement for customer loyalty? What are they?
  - Return Policies
    - > What are your return policies? Are receipts required? How many days? What condition?
  - Warranty
    - > What is your warranty on your product or service? Length of time? Other conditions? Receipt required?
    - > How will you handle warranty issues?
- Training
  - Describe your employee customer service training.
  - How long does initial training last?
  - Ongoing training – how often?
  - What is your philosophy regarding customer service?
- Feedback
  - Do you have any methods or procedures for gathering feedback from customers?
  - How do you process that feedback and how do you implement change from it?
  - Customer Surveys
    - > Do you conduct customer surveys?
    - > How often are they done?
    - > How are they done?
    - > What does it consist of?
    - > How do you measure the results?
    - > Who is included in the surveys?

12. Logistics
- Inventory Management
  - Will you use LIFO or FIFO? How will you manage inventory

to avoid cash flow problems? What levels of inventory will you carry? Do your suppliers always have a ready supply of replacement inventory?

- Distribution
  - Shipping Contracts
    - \> Identify the types of contracts available and the benefits and restrictions of each. Who is the best shipping company for your needs?
  - Shipping Supplies
    - \> Identify sources for shipping supplies. What type of supplies will you use and the estimated costs?

13. Launch Strategy

- Press Release
  - \> Where will you submit them? Draft an example of your press release. How will you get the press to pick it up?
- Soft Launch
  - \> Why and how will you accomplish a soft launch? How long between the soft launch and the grand opening?
- Grand Opening
  - \> Describe in detail the grand opening events, how you will promote it, how many days it will last, and what specials you will offer.

14. Strategic Planning

- Mission Statement
  - Does the operation of your business resemble your mission statement? If not, why not? What are your core values?
- Growth Model
  - What are your plans for expansion at your existing location? Or, if your model is online, how does it grow? What about additional location or adding new product's and/or services?
- Sustainability
  - What systems are in place to ensure your business can identify trends and make timely adjustments to remain viable in your market?

15. Exit Strategy

- IPO
  - Can your business grow to the size of eventually making a public offering of your stock?

- Selling the Business
  - What are your plans for eventually selling the business? Will it be to family or to employees? Or will it be offered through a business broker?
- Franchising
  - Is this a goal for you? What level of success will you need to reach before this becomes a viable option? What level of financing will be required and what is the true potential of you venture being replicated in other markets?
- Licensing
  - Does this alternative to franchising have any possibilities for your type of business? What are the factors that determine whether licensing or franchising is appropriate for the offering you want to make?
- Merge
  - Will it benefit you to allow your business to be merged into another? Is it possible to merge another business into yours?
- Pass Down to Family
  - Have you clearly determined and documented a clear line of succession within the family? Will this plan endure the longevity of the business with the least amount of disruption?
- Liquidation
  - Will you use a liquidation service? Are there any other alternatives to optimize the revenue generated from this process?

I hate it when people say an entrepreneur is "someone who jumps off a cliff (or out of an airplane) and builds a parachute on the way down." It's ridiculous. Countless numbers of entrepreneurs are remarkably sane, and no sane person makes that jump expecting to successfully build a parachute before hitting the ground.

While I very much agree with the lean startup philosophy and shy away from writing formal business plans unless some funding mechanism requires them, understanding and thinking through the concepts in Nelson's 15-point roadmap is something any smart entrepreneur or investor does. Adam Whitney, a former student of mine as well as Nelson's, just launched his second venture, Enigma Creative Group. Via email Adam told me, "I use [Nelson's] road map every day... Running a business is complicated, hard and even scary some days, but the lessons I learned building the road map make it easier. Although I don't keep a copy in front of me every day, I have studied it enough to apply it to my process of making business decisions." Adam is just one of many students-turned-entrepreneurs who personally told me how valuable they found the roadmap process to be after they had graduated and launched their ventures.

Bibliography

Introduction
- How Colleges are Becoming Entrepreneurial: http://techcrunch.com/2012/07/08/how-colleges-are-becoming-entrepreneurial/
- Philip J. Patiño School of Entrepreneurship: http://www.fresnobee.com/opinion/article23052462.html
- Florida State School for Entrepreneurship Announcement: http://news.fsu.edu/Top-Stories/FSU-receives-100M-to-create-the-Jim-Moran-School-of-Entrepreneurship

Coming Up With an Idea – Avoid the Obvious Paths
- Hult Prize: http://www.hultprize.org
- Hult Prize 2015 Finals: http://livestream.com/hultprize/2015awarddinner/videos/100585711
- Tembo: http://www.temboeducationgroup.com

Startup Internships
- Should you intern at startups?: http://www.livemint.com/Leisure/9xsBN0YWl6PRxiX2nQ3fmK/Should-you-intern-at-startups.html

Picking a Startup Team
- Three Asses Rule: http://softtechvc.com/strategy/about-us/
- Trudeau's World Economic Forum Address: http://www.huffingtonpost.ca/2016/01/20/justin-trudeau-waterloo-humblebrag_n_9032006.html
- McKinsey & Company Diversity Findings: http://www.mckinsey.com/Insights/Organization/Why_diversity_matters

It's OK to Get a Job...
- Hey, entrepreneurs: Get a job: http://venturebeat.com/2015/04/04/hey-entrepreneurs-get-a-job/
- 2015 Gallup Data: http://tinyurl.com/gr2lgdm

I Am a CEO
- Your body language shapes who you are (#2 most viewed TED Talk of all time): http://www.ted.com/talks/amy_cuddy_your_body_language_shapes_who_you_are?language=en
- Amy Cuddy takes a stand: http://www.nytimes.com/2014/09/21/

fashion/amy-cuddy-takes-a-stand-TED-talk.html?_r=0
- The 3x5 rule: http://www.entrepreneur.com/article/242763
- Priestley, D. (2010). Become a Key Person of Influence. Ecademy Press.

You Are Not Special
- National Center for Education Statistics: https://nces.ed.gov/fastfacts/display.asp?id=84
- Steve Jobs' 2005 Stanford Commencement Address: http://news.stanford.edu/news/2005/june15/jobs-061505.html
- Jim Carrey's 2014 MUM Commencement Address: https://www.youtube.com/watch?v=V80-gPkpH6M
- David McCullough's 2012 Wellesley Commencement Address: https://www.youtube.com/watch?v=_lfxYhtf8o4
- Admiral William H. McRaven's 2014 UT Austin Commencement Address: http://news.utexas.edu/2014/05/16/admiral-mcraven-commencement-speech
- Oprah Winfrey's 2013 Harvard Commencement Speech: http://news.harvard.edu/gazette/story/2013/05/winfreys-commencement-address/?utm_source=youtube&utm_medium=social&utm_campaign=hu-youtube-card

Get Gritty
- Grit: https://www.youtube.com/watch?v=H14bBuluwB8
- Helping Students Succeed by Building Grit: http://www.carnegiefoundation.org/blog/helping-students-succeed-by-building-grit/
- Angela Lee Duckworth's Grit TED Talk: https://www.ted.com/talks/angela_lee_duckworth_the_key_to_success_grit?language=en
- Carol Dweck's Growth Mindset TED Talk: https://www.ted.com/talks/carol_dweck_the_power_of_believing_that_you_can_improve?language=en
- Ericsson, K. A., Krampe, R. T., & Tesch-Römer, C. (1993). The role of deliberate practice in the acquisition of expert performance. Psychological Review, 100(3), 363-406.

Arrogance + Entrepreneurship
- Ideasphere: http://ideasphere.com/

Become Rejection Proof

- Jason Comely's Website: www.rejectiontherapy.com
- Jia Jiang's Website: www.fearbuster.com
- Jiang, J. (2015). Rejection Proof. New York: Harmony Books.

Beer, Sex, and Bricolage

- Mobcraft Beer: https://www.mobcraftbeer.com
- Scanalytics Incorporated: http://www.scanalyticsinc.com
- Weick, K.E. (2001). Making Sense of Organizations. Malden, MA: Blackwell.
- Neck, H.M., Greene, P.G., & Brush, C.G. (2014). Teaching entrepreneurship: A practice-based approach. Edward Elgar Publishing.

Backpack Entrepreneurship

- Backpack Entrepreneurs Online Community and Podcast: http://backpackentrepreneurs.com
- Jay Meistrich's How I Built a Startup While Travelling to 20 Countries: http://www.entrepreneur.com/article/241761

Six Questions to Answer Before Starting Up

- Why 90% of Startups Fail: http://mashable.com/2013/02/04/why-startups-fail/

90 Seconds of Fame (aka Your 90-Second Pitch)

- Business Insider Study: http://www.businessinsider.com/only-7-seconds-to-make-first-impression-2013-4
- Microsoft Attention Span Report: http://advertising.microsoft.com/en/cl/31966/how-does-digital-affect-canadian-attention-spans

Purposeful Networking

- Bridges, B. (2013). Networking on Purpose: A Five-Part Success Plan to Build a Powerful and Profitable Business Network. Fresno, CA: iBridge Enterprises.

Waiting for Perfect When Good Will Do

- Freedman, D. H. (2001). Corps business: The 30 management principles of the US Marines. New York: HarperBusiness.
- Louis C.K. GQ Interview: http://www.gq.com/story/louis-ck-cover-story-may-2014?currentPage=1

So You Want to Open a Restaurant...

- The 39 Most Iconic College Town Food Joints Across North America: http://www.huffingtonpost.com/spoon-university/the-39-most-iconic-college-town-food-joints-across-north-america_b_6928480.html

Learn to Sell

- Pandora.com's Investor Pitch Statistic: http://www.entrepreneur.com/article/228438
- Gone With The Wind Rejection Statistic: http://www.litrejections.com/best-sellers-initially-rejected/
- Jordan, M. (2012). Driven from within. Simon and Schuster.

The Deal with Accelerators

- AngelList: http://angel.co
- Boost Accelerator Program: http://Boost.VC
- Simon Sinek TED Talk: https://www.ted.com/talks/simon_sinek_how_great_leaders_inspire_action?language=en

What Successful Entrepreneurs Think You Should Read

- Lewis, M. (2004). Moneyball: The art of winning an unfair game. WW Norton & Company.
- Kim, W. C., & Mauborgne, R. (2015). Blue Ocean Strategy, Expanded Edition: How to Create Uncontested Market Space and Make the Competition Irrelevant. Harvard Business Review Press.
- Kaplan, R. S. (2011). What to ask the person in the mirror: Critical questions for becoming a more effective leader and reaching your potential. Harvard Business Press.
- Brown, D. J. (2013). The boys in the boat: Nine Americans and their epic quest for gold at the 1936 Berlin Olympics. Penguin.
- Wickman, G. (2012). Traction: Get a Grip on Your Business. BenBella Books, Inc.
- Berger, J. (2013). Contagious: Why things catch on. Simon and Schuster.
- Jonah Berger's "Contagious: Why Things Catch On" Talk at Google: https://www.youtube.com/watch?v=FN4eDk1pq6U

About the Author

Dr. Eric Liguori is a professor in the John P. Lowth Entrepreneurship Center at The University of Tampa. He also teaches innovation and entrepreneurship in Aalto University's Global Bachelor's Program in International Business. Liguori works daily to help students and startups succeed. He's on the U.S. Association for Small Business and Entrepreneurship's Board of Directors, the National Faculty Advisory Council of the Collegiate Entrepreneurs' Organization, is Co-Director of the Entrepreneurship Education Project, and is a Startup Weekend, Startup Week, and 1 Million Cups Community Organizer in Tampa, FL. Liguori's been quoted or featured in *USA Today, Publisher's Weekly, The Tampa Tribune, The Business Journal,* and on *Forbes. com, Monster.com, Digiday.com,* ABC30, and LinkedIn Pulse.

Liguori is the recipient of the 2014 Lyles Center Entrepreneurship Education Excellence Award, a student-chosen award given to the individual who has made the largest impact in the lives of entrepreneurship students. He is also the recipient of the 2015 Small Business Institute Best Conceptual Research Paper Award, the 2014 Southern Management Association Outstanding Strategy Paper Award, and took 3rd place in the Center for Entrepreneurial Excellence's 2012 National Experiential Entrepreneurship Education Competition. While proud of these accomplishments, he is more proud of these incredible achievements of his students:

- 1st Place, Global Startup Battle's Disruptors & Big Ideas Track (2015)
- 1st Place, Startup Weekend Tampa Bay (2015)
- 3rd Place, Startup Weekend Tampa Bay (2015)
- 3rd Place, Veterans Business Symposium Business Plan Competition (2015)
- Top 50 Finalists (out of 20,000+ global teams), Hult Prize Competition (2015)
- Spencer Award for Entrepreneurial Excellence (2012, 2013, 2014, 2015)
- 1st Place Nationally, Campus E-Diffusion, CEO Fresno Chapter (2013)
- Fresno Chamber of Commerce College Entrepreneur of the Year (2012, 2013)
- Sandler Training Presidents Club Scholarship (2013)
- Sandler Training Sales Fundamentals Scholarship (2013)
- CEO Startup Simulation Challenge Finalist Team (2012)

In their own words, here is what Liguori's students have to say about him:

"Professor Liguori is, bar none, the best professor I have had in my college career. He has been an absolute game-changer for me and the direction of my business. He is completely dedicated to each and every student and will stop at nothing to help one achieve the goals set ahead of them."

– Laura Facciani Sanford
Class of 2013

"Dr. Liguori is by far one of the best professors I've had the honor of meeting outside of the classroom. His overall enthusiasm and drive keep him busy and he never avoids a challenge. He is very friendly and knows exactly what he's talking about. By far one of the most influential people in my life!"

– Gurbhupinder "Gary" Sahota
Class of 2013

"Dr. Eric Liguori has truly facilitated entrepreneurship inside the Fresno State campus, more so than anybody else. Whether organizing a global event like Startup Weekend or leading Fresno State's Collegiate Entrepreneurs' Organization (CEO) to numerous national awards, Eric has helped foster a culture of innovation and entrepreneurship inside the Fresno State campus. In a school better known for its achievements in the agricultural industry, Eric has inspired a movement in entrepreneurial education that has seen a number of student-run businesses take off."

– Renan de Lima
Class of 2015

Liguori can be reached via the following:
- LinkedIn: https://www.linkedin.com/in/eliguori
- Twitter: @ericliguori
- Personal Website: www.eliguori.com
- Email: info@thestartupstudent.co